Communicating Emotion at Work

Vincent R. Waldron

polity

First published in 2012 by Polity Press

Polity Press
65 Bridge Street
Cambridge CB2 1UR, UK

Polity Press
350 Main Street
Malden, MA 02148, USA

ISBN-13: 978-0-7456-4895-8
ISBN-13: 978-0-7456-4896-5(pb)

A catalogue record for this book is available from the British Library.

Typeset in 11 on 13 pt Sabon
by Servis Filmsetting Ltd, Stockport, Cheshire
Printed and bound in Great Britain by the MPG Books Group

The publisher has used its best endeavours to ensure that the URLs for external websites referred to in this book are correct and active at the time of going to press. However, the publisher has no responsibility for the websites and can make no guarantee that a site will remain live or that the content is or will remain appropriate.

Every effort has been made to trace all copyright holders, but if any have been inadvertently overlooked the publisher will be pleased to include any necessary credits in any subsequent reprint or edition.

For further information on Polity, visit our website: www.politybooks.com

Contents

Contents

Contents

Contents

Figures and Tables

Figures

Tables

Preface

In recent years, researchers of communication and organizational behavior have become intensely interested in the communication of emotion at work. This interest is also evident in our classrooms, as those of us who teach courses in organizational communication or organizational behavior pay more attention to the topic. At research conferences, audiences pack those sessions that address the emotional experiences of workers. Why the interest? Several reasons come to mind. First, researchers have documented the importance of emotional communication practices in a startling array of occupations: healthcare providers, teachers, managers, detectives, airline attendants, emergency responders, salespeople, public relations specialists, and even sex workers, among so many others. Second, despite cultural norms that discourage workplace emotionality, nearly all workers recall vivid and career-changing emotional experiences. One might recall the intense feelings of camaraderie and pride that attended the successful completion of a grueling team project. Another remembers feelings of burning indignation when a team member unfairly took credit for the work she completed. Yet another recollects feelings of anger and fear when confronted with a bullying boss or a harassing co-worker. Feelings of admiration, frustration, awe, grief, joy, and glee – these too are memorable markers on the emotional landscape of a career.

Another, third, reason for the interest is that emotional experiences mark meaningful episodes in working lives that might otherwise be routine, regulated, and mundane. Experiences become emotional because they *matter*. We get emotional when our peers support us through difficult moments or our work identity comes under unexpected attack. Our emotions signal danger. They tell us when our career is at risk or our values are under attack. But they also bond us to leaders and colleagues in enriching, supportive, and lasting relationships. Organizations that tend to the emotional climate of the workplace are more likely to detect lapses in ethical conduct and to redress sagging employee morale. In all of these ways, the communication of emotion creates important meanings for employees and their organizations.

Finally, emotion interests us because it is often a *communicative* experience. Certainly, emotion is a psychological and biological phenomenon. But it is through communication that emotion is recognized in others, expressed, regulated, interpreted, and elicited. The communication of emotion is an important competency for workers, their leaders, and organizations. Emotional norms are communicated via popular media, including reality TV shows such as *The Apprentice* and "mockumentaries" such as *The Office*. Communication technologies such as Facebook, video-conferencing, and even email can inhibit and enhance emotional communication. Finally, emotion is communicative in that larger cultural and economic discourses shape the emotional experiences of employees – through gender roles, definitions of heroism and leadership, the degree to which feelings associated with work are discounted or granted economic value, and many other factors.

The Approach: Research-Grounded, Theory-Guided, Example-Driven

The book is grounded in the author's own research and that of other emotion researchers. Students are exposed to key contributions by scholars of organizational behavior, management, psychology, and organizational communication. Each chapter shares the lived experiences of working people – as collected through surveys, interviews, and the author's own observations.

Some of the examples are based on the experiences of my students, many of whom work full or part time. In all cases, names and identifying details are fictionalized to protect the identities of those involved. Readers will hear from probation officers, factory workers, teachers, salespeople, managers, customer service representatives, social workers, and engineers, among others. They will hear family members describe how the emotional nature of work influences their personal lives. Where illustrative, I draw from my own experiences working in a variety of corporate and university settings.

Keeping in mind the undergraduate reader, the text is rich in examples and applications: rich quotations from working people; references to popular media programs and significant news stories; brief case analyses; and summaries of interesting or foundational research studies. Each chapter begins with a stimulating quotation, narrative, or question. Always, the focus is squarely on communication and the concepts that student readers will encounter in their courses.

How is the Book Organized?

Communicating Emotion at Work begins with an accessible introduction to the study of emotion in the workplace. In chapter 1, students learn that emotional communication has been an interest of scholars for literally thousands of years. The emotionally unique features of work are discussed as are some of the seminal studies of emotional labor. The chapter familiarizes readers with different conceptualizations of emotion and the recent emphasis on "positive" emotions. Ultimately, chapter 1 makes the case that emotional communication plays a crucial, humanizing, and constructive role as employees perform tasks, make meaning, forge healthy and just relationships, and navigate the requirements of work, family, and culture. In a variety of ways, emotional communication helps employees and organizations do *good*.

Chapter 2 is all about communication. It examines the functions of emotional communication at various levels of organizations –

individual, relational, workgroup, organizational, occupational, societal, and global. The second half of the chapter delineates the many and rich forms of emotional communication in the workplace. I consider non-verbal cues, emotion words, metaphors, stories, interaction patterns, rituals, externally directed organizational messages, and many others. Chapter 3 chronicles an interesting assortment of emotional occupations. Students will read about the emotional labors of crisis workers and con artists, salespeople and sports coaches, secretaries and religious leaders.

Chapter 4 explains how communication processes get played out as work relationships are nurtured, maintained, and terminated. The emotional requirements of leadership and followership receive attention. Supportive and troubled peer relationships are discussed as are some less familiar relational bonds, including creative teams, partnerships, and workplace romances. Chapter 5 focuses attention on the ethical dimensions of emotional communication at work. The important contributions of the "moral emotions" are explored, with particular attention given to such feelings of guilt, pride, envy, and embarrassment. Emotional communication is depicted as an important check on immoral practices and a contributor to just work relationships. The immoral communication tactics of "emotional tyrants" are detailed, as are the sometimes unintended moral consequences of organizational procedures and communication practices.

Communicating Emotion at Work ends with a look at the societal and economic trends that are shaping the emotional lives of workers. Among these are round-the-clock connectivity, the rise of temporary work arrangements, occupational trends, new products and services, and the role of forgiveness in redressing hurt and wrongdoing at work. As is the case throughout this book, the possibilities of emotional exploitation are fully acknowledged, but the productive, ethical, and humanizing aspects of emotional communication are embraced. *Communicating Emotion at Work* makes the case that communication of feeling is not only necessary at work; it is often good.

Acknowledgments

The study of emotion at work has interested me since my days as a PhD student at Ohio State in the late 1980s. Due to the demands of my other research interests and responsibilities, I have had the pleasure of writing on the topic only sporadically over the years. Nonetheless, my passion has never abated, due largely to the continuous stream of intriguing studies, stimulating conversations, and supportive messages provided by colleagues in the discipline. Some of these exchanges occurred long ago and others are of more recent vintage.

Kathleen Krone was among my first mentors and we co-authored one of the earlier studies on the communication of emotion at work – a rewarding experience that I still remember with fondness. Although we speak only rarely, over the years I have deeply appreciated her quiet support, stimulating research questions, good humor, and humane approach to the work of teaching and researching. As a graduate student and young professor, I had the opportunity to chat with Linda Putnam on a variety of occasions about our mutual interest in workplace emotions. Her encouragement during those early years convinced me that I was on to something important, something worth studying for the long run. Thanks, Linda. In 1999, Sally Planalp wrote an important book on communication and emotion – one that inspired me to try the same thing one day. Although her understanding of emotion far exceeds mine, that day has finally arrived.

More recently, I have had the pleasure of working at the same institution (Arizona State University) with Sarah Tracy, whose research on workplace emotion continues to be prolific, thought-provoking, and useful to real-life workers and my own students. I met Pamela Lutgen-Sandvik in one of Sarah's doctoral seminars some years ago. Pam's research is fresh, inspiring, and grounded in an assumption that I think we share: that the nature of emotional communication is an important indicator of the degree to which a workplace community is healthy, ethical, and humane.

Various other scholars have offered collegial support or inspiration over the many years that I have been contemplating this project. To name just a few: Ted Zorn, Jeff Kassing, Patricia Sias, Don Cegala.

My deepest thanks go to all of the many students who shared their emotional work experiences in class. More than anything else, their stories keep me thinking about the power of emotional communication at work.

Josh Danaher, my former student and co-author on the "Emotional Occupations" chapter, proved to be an inquisitive, hard-working, and patient collaborator. Josh has a bright future as a communication educator and I am grateful for his help.

Finally, as always, I thank my wife Kathleen for her invaluable help as I work though my most challenging tasks, which include, appropriately enough, communicating emotion at work.

1

Emotional Connections

Intersections of Communication, Work, and Feeling

> Ryan was a senior manager who kept two fishbowls in his office. In one were goldfish; in the other, a piranha. Ryan asked each of his staff to pick out the goldfish that was most like themselves (the spotted one, the one with the deeper color and so forth). Then, when Ryan was displeased with someone, he would ask that person to take his or her goldfish out of the bowl and feed it to the piranha.
>
> Frost, 2003: 35

This rather chilling tale, shared by organizational scholar Peter Frost, illustrates vividly how communication and emotion are so richly and complexly intertwined in organizations. Ryan appears to be a tyrannical manager with a taste for fish-sacrificing ritual, but only a few unfortunate employees will come to know this through direct observation. The vast majority will learn about Ryan's terrorizing ways through communication. It will be a co-worker's telling of the story that strikes fear in their hearts. Indeed, we can imagine shudders of emotion rippling down the hallways as this fishy tale flows ever further from Ryan's office. Wide-eyed colleagues will gather around the office coffee pot, gasping as they hear the story for the first time. What feelings will they share during those hushed conversations? *Relief* in the knowledge that "my fish" has yet to be terrorized? *Anger* at upper management's failure to curb Ryan's over-the-top antics? *Guilt* about their own efforts to ingratiate themselves with Ryan, hoping to remain in his good graces and out of the piranha's lair? *Fear* of what the future may bring? Mutual *pride* at their capacity to thrive in a "survival-of-the-fittest" organizational culture? As the story is told and then retold, emotion will be created collectively: expressed, interpreted, labeled, modified, magnified, and remembered.

As the tale of Ryan's fish-slaughtering proclivities sinks deeper into the emotional tissues of this organization, we can imagine that it will manifest itself in a myriad of communicative effects, some of them completely unintended. Like a good horror movie it may prove deliciously scary to its employee "audience," a source of emotional bonding and entertainment on days when the work is dull and feelings of camaraderie have dissipated. Alternatively, veteran workers may delight in using the story to alarm naive newcomers. By telling it with bravado, or even indifference, the senior members model organizationally expected emotions, even as they cultivate emotional hardiness in envious neophytes. This type of informal socialization may help the rookies negotiate the tricky emotional terrain of leader–member relationships. Finally, structures of power and control will be supported or challenged by emotional reactions to the piranha story. Fear may silence Ryan's critics and encourage them to support his goals and tactics. Conversely, feelings of outrage or indignation could motivate employees to resist or complain. And, of course, employees who feel disgusted may simply seek a more emotionally nurturing organizational culture.

The Ubiquity of Emotional Communication

Emotional communication has been the subject of intense study for thousands of years. In the Western tradition we see it emerging in the philosophical writings of Aristotle (trans. 2000), and the advice offered by Cicero (trans. 2001), the influential political orator of ancient Rome. Both of these influential thinkers recognized the power of emotional appeals in moving an audience but worried over the moral implications of doing so. Many years later, scientific interest in emotion was ignited by the work of Charles Darwin (1872/1998) who posited that expressions of emotions evolved as a way to promote cooperation among animals living in complex social groupings. Modern psychologists have come to view emotion as one of the key motivational drivers of social behavior (e.g., Keltner, 2009; Weiner, 2006) and scholars have examined the many connections between emotion and communication behaviors (Bolls, 2010; Burleson, 2003, 2008; Metts and Wood, 2008; Planalp, 1999; Nabi, 2010). In recent decades, writers from a variety of disciplines have explored the rich and vital role of emotional communication practices in sustaining organizations and institutions (e.g., Dougherty and Krone, 2002; Hochschild, 1979, 1983; Fineman, 2000; Frost, 2003; Krone and Morgan, 2000; Miller, Considine, and Garner, 2007; Tracy and Tracy, 1998; Mumby and Putnam, 1992; Waldron, 1994). So, in the complicated story of how humans organize their behavior, emotional communication has always played an important role.

And, as any casual observer quickly realizes, the communication of emotion is a pervasive, and sometimes unfortunate, feature of Western popular culture. Who hasn't cringed at the public humiliation of the hopeful but often hapless contestants on wildly popular televised talent shows such as *Britain's Got Talent* or *American Idol*. Indeed, a staple of the genre is the emotionally blistering critique offered by an apparently hard-hearted celebrity judge. At the same time, these programs play with the viewers' emotions by featuring maudlin performances and ever-building suspense. And the season is often punctuated with a surprising emotional wallop, as in 2009, when an unassuming middle-aged amateur named Susan Boyle stunned the judges and brought the audience to tears with soaring vocal performances. Emotional communication is also the main attraction of a seemingly endless parade of popular daytime talk shows, with hosts encouraging "celebrity" guests to bare their souls, confess their sins, and express whatever feelings they can conjure up on the spot – all to the delight of a studio audience which often participates in the emotionfest by hissing, applauding, and emitting sympathetic noises.

Five Types of Organizational Emotion

Against this over-the-top cultural backdrop it would be easy to miss the important role that emotional communication plays in the workplace. In fact, we might assume that popular culture is the outlet for emotions that we are prevented from expressing at work. Indeed, for many years scholars considered the workplace something of an emotional dead zone. After all, "getting emotional" has long been considered unprofessional in many organizations, and much of the early organizational research examined relatively bland and undifferentiated emotional states such as low morale or high job satisfaction. Emotion was simply a by-product of more important factors, like wages or supervision practices. But this simplified conceptualization has been enriched in recent years, as researchers have come to learn what many employees knew all along: that the expression of emotion is an integral part of the tasks workers perform, the relationships they sustain, and the meanings they derive from work.

Katherine Miller, a prominent organizational communication researcher, proposes five types of organizational emotion. She and several colleagues identified these five themes in stories told by workers employed in a large variety of occupations (Miller et al., 2007). The narratives were reported originally in the books *Working* (Terkel, 1974) and *Gig* (Bowe, Bowe, and Streeter, 2000). I have adapted the types below, based on my own studies of various workplaces. Each type raises important questions for communication researchers and for workers (table 1.1).

Emotional labor and surface acting

Emotional communication is an integral part of the work performed by employees who get paid to do what researchers have come to call *emotional labor*. Here, Miller and her colleagues (2007) draw on the pioneering work of Arlie Hochschild (1983), a sociologist who spent many hours observing airline attendants, restaurant servers, and other service professionals. Hochschild soon noticed that much of the labor performed by attendants

Table 1.1 Selected questions about emotional communication in the workplace

___

Surface acting
- What kinds of emotions must be fabricated to perform the job?
- How are these emotions displayed verbally and non-verbally?
- What are the communication rules and role requirements that regulate emotional displays? How do display rules change across organizations, occupations, and cultures?
- What processes of socialization help employees learn these emotional display rules?
- How does surface acting help or hinder the performance of employees and their organizations?
- Does surface acting harm employees or those who interact with them?

Deep acting
- What emotions do employees feel on the job?
- How do employees learn to feel authentic emotions in the course of their work?
- What organizational processes are used to cultivate and control employee emotion?
- How do employees express the emotions that are banned by the organization?
- What are the consequences of deep acting for employees?

Relational emotion
- Which emotion words are used to define working relationships and co-workers?
- What forms of emotional communication are expected of co-workers?
- How does the expression of emotions sustain or change relationships?
- How is emotional communication used to assert or resist power?
- How does emotion flow across formal and informal networks?
- How do employees cooperate to produce collective emotion?

Emotional boundary spanning
- How do emotions cross the fluid boundaries between work and home?
- How do societal norms affect the expression of emotion at work?
- How do organizations incorporate emotion in their public messages?

Emotional effects
- How do workers describe the emotional effects of their work to others?
- What kinds of work are experienced as joyful and fulfilling?

Table 1.1   (continued)

- Which occupations experience high rates of emotional burnout?
- How do emotional effects of work change over the course of a career?
- How are the emotional effects of work addressed by organizations?
- In what ways do employees actively manage emotional effects?

involved displays of inauthentic emotion, a process she called *surface acting*. In service work (and, to some lesser degree, nearly every profession), the production of emotion is not simply a reaction to work. It *is* the work.

At the time of Hochschild's data collection (the 1970s), airline attendants were exclusively female. They were trained to exhibit cheerfulness at all times, even when responding to passengers who were rude, cranky, frightened, or sexually aggressive. In the hiring process, attendants were selected for their bubbly personalities and they received intensive training in the arts of emotional fabrication. In today's economy, surface acting is perhaps the most crucial communicative requirement of our many service jobs. Consider Walmart greeters who produce a continuous stream of welcoming smiles for customers, even when they feel bored and listless, or the car salesperson who is required to manufacture enthusiasm for even the lowliest of clunkers hidden at the back of the lot. Surface acting is crucial in other less obvious occupational contexts. What would be the consequence if a weary funeral director failed to muster expressions of sympathy? Or if a nervous young emergency-room physician could not project a sense of calm? Or if a president admitted to being discouraged rather than hopeful about the country's economic prospects? In each of these cases, communication is the means by which "real feelings" are repackaged or inauthentic feelings are created for public consumption (Waldron, 1994).

Emotional work and deep acting

A second category is called *emotional work* (Miller et al., 2007). Here the work itself is emotional and the feelings are authentic.

Social work may create feelings of compassion and, in some cases, futility. Religious work produces feelings of awe or dread before God. Military work involves feelings of patriotism and, under some conditions, fear. The work of political activists involves indignation and hope. These real feelings occur spontaneously as people become immersed in their labor, or they may be cultivated over time. This second variation on the theme is what Hochschild (1983) called *deep acting*, when employees internalize and come to "own" the feelings they are expected to have on the job. For example, Hochschild's flight attendants used tricks of imagination to help them feel sympathy rather than annoyance when confronted with grumpy passengers. They were trained to imagine that the customer had just experienced a tragedy, had a terrible day at the office, or was terrified of a plane crash.

Organizations go to great lengths to help employees genuinely feel emotions. One of the most studied is Disney (e.g., Van Mannen and Kunda, 1989) with its widely emulated training programs, in which each theme-park employee is "cast" in the Disney show. In viewing themselves not as janitors, or ride operators, or cashiers, but as actors, Disney employees are encouraged to develop a deep emotional commitment to the company and fellow cast members, and they may feel gratitude for the opportunity to perform in front of a customer "audience." Faced with thousands of tired and sometimes impatient visitors, Disney employees learn not to feel impatience or indignation when they are mistreated.

However, emotional communication sometimes varies from the organizational script, as sociologists Van Maanen and Kunda revealed in their seminal field study with Disney workers (1989). When exacerbated by particularly rude or combative guests, Disney ride operators have been known to extract sweet revenge, using a tactic known as the "seatbelt squeeze." The offending visitor is obligingly ushered into his or her seat by one operator. Then, under the pretense of safety, a co-worker deliberately yanks the seatbelt until it is cinched painfully around the offender's waist. This is not the kind of heartfelt performance that Disney trainers have in mind. But the maneuver is certainly an expression of authentic emotion. It demonstrates that customer-service work is truly emotional work, not just an emotional fabrication. Further, the evolution of the seatbelt squeeze is evidence that, despite the formal efforts of organizations to shape their emotional lives, employees' real feelings also stem from participation in the informal organizational cultural – in this case, one which encourages hostility to be expressed in clandestine, collaborative, and creative forms of communication.

Relational emotion

Relational emotion, or what Miller et al. (2007) called *emotion with work*, arises from interactions with co-workers. For example, encounters with workplace bullies may cause emotional distress (Lutgen-Sandvik, Namie, and Namie, 2009) or, more positively, interactions among co-workers may result in feelings of affection and shared pride. High-status employees sometimes elicit emotions such as fear as they consolidate their power (Waldron, 2009). And employees often cooperate to produce emotions, as when team members gather after work to share amusing stories and vent their shared frustrations. Finally, co-workers use emotion words to describe those with whom they work, using labels such as "bubbly," "moody," "volcanic," and "calming."

Emotional boundary spanning

A fourth type of emotion is that which crosses the fluid boundaries of organizations. Miller and colleagues (2007) use the term *emotion at work* in reference to the ways in which employees bring emotions from home to work (see also Judge, Ilies, and Scott, 2005). The employee who grieves the death of a family member and shares the loss with co-workers is one example. But boundaries are also breeched by larger social and cultural norms that shape employee expectations about emotional communication. What is "normal" emotional behavior for men and women? Or for the powerful and unempowered? For those serving customers and by the customers themselves? Finally, organizations employ a whole class of professional boundary spanners to help them elicit emotions from the public. These people work in public relations, crises management, advertising, and similar occupations.

Emotional effects

Finally, most employees experience what Miller et al. (2007) call *emotion toward work*. These are emotional effects or consequences of working. Employees communicate them using a variety of familiar terms. Some will feel joy toward their tasks, pride in their accomplishments, and emotionally fulfilled by their careers. Others will feel dread at the beginning of each work week, burned-out by job demands, or emotionally drained by their interactions with colleagues or clients. However, it would be a mistake to assume that employees are passive, helpless victims of their emotions. They often take action to modulate or change these effects, to use them in their own interests.

Communication researcher Sarah Tracy was thinking in this way when she questioned traditional notions of emotional burnout in a recent essay (2009). Tracy introduces the idea of engagement – the degree and type of investment employees are willing to make. Some workers creatively disengage as a way of managing their exposure to negative emotional experiences. Rather than passive recipients of unrelenting occupational stress, they can be viewed as active responders who are making psychological adjustments and altering communication practices. They do so to preserve emotional resources and manage their exposure to stressors. To ward off emotional exhaustion, they may temporarily downgrade their expectations and invest themselves where it will do the most good. Of course, these individual actions can go only so far in environments that are deeply and persistently emotionally toxic. Changes in organizational practices and supervisory practices are likely to be more impactful. Yet, for the emotionally savvy employee, these adjustments could foster resilience and keep them on the job longer.

Why Take an Organizational Communication Perspective?

Emotion in the workplace is often studied by psychologists, who generally view emotion as a biological and psychological response to environmental stimuli (Sandelands and Boudens, 2000). How do individuals respond to workplace conditions and assess them, and how do these assessments motivate action? As I note below, psychologists increasingly take a biological and evolutionary view of emotion (for example, Keltner, 2009). How does emotion help an organism, in this case an employee, survive in a difficult environment? In contrast, management researchers and practitioners study emotion with concern for the organization's goals. How can organizational variables be adjusted to create desired emotional response in employees or customers? In this view, emotion is an organizational resource or an employee competency. Emotional "assets" can be cultivated through careful employee selection, training, and effective management. Finally, the field of organization studies tends to view organizational life as an expression of larger cultural and economic forces. Unlike psychobiological theorists, these researchers view emotion as a *social construction*. They wonder how employees make meaning from emotional experiences, given their interactions with others and their participation in larger systems of meaning, such as ethnic cultures and economic systems. For them, emotion is social. These theorists look closely at the language practices and cultural conventions that seem to create certain emotional experiences, such as pride, shame, or moral outrage.

So what does it mean to view emotion from a communication perspective in general, and an organizational communication perspective, in particular? First, I want to be clear that some communication scholars fall into all three of the camps described above: biopsychological, managerial, and social constructionist. But, as chapter 2 discusses in more detail, communication researchers study the messages, interactions, and structures that people (and collectives) use in their efforts to create meanings, coordinate activities, and advance their goals. To put it simply, their focus is on understanding communication processes more than individual reactions or organizational assets. Communication is enacted in specific contexts, such as families, friendships, and, most important here, workplaces. The organizational context has unique features, some of which shape the way that emotion is communicated (Planalp, 1999; Waldron, 1994). For example, the tasks that people perform at the behest of their organizations assure that certain kinds of communication qualities, including emotional ones, will be valued. In addition, communication at work is structured by rules, reporting relationships, and role requirements, some of which regulate the expression of emotion. Another factor is power, which is concentrated in some parts of organizations. Powerful people are better able to use emotional communication to the advantage of themselves and their organizations. Finally, organizations are nested within larger systems, such as communities, economies, and cultures, and must be responsive to their emotional norms and needs.

From this discussion, we can see that emotional communication is subject to organizational constraints, some of which individual employees are not aware of and many of which are beyond their control. Yet communication is an inherently creative process and it is through communication that employees discover, interpret, enact, resist, and negotiate organizational controls. It is the means by which individual and organizational goals are negotiated and a meaningful working life is defined. Emotional communication is among the most valuable and potent of the symbolic tools used for these purposes. This brief case study illustrates the point.

The Case of the Emotional School Teacher

Alejandra is a mid-career science teacher known for her classroom enthusiasm, inventive teaching methods, and unfailing belief that each of her seventh-grade students will share the awe she feels when confronted by the wonders of nature. Alejandra feels pride at the praise she receives from grateful parents. Admired by most of her colleagues, Alejandra is also resented by others who are turned off by her "over-the-top" commitment of evening and weekend hours to her teaching tasks. But now, more than a decade into her teaching career, Alejandra admits that she has learned to "stop caring quite so much." Disappointed by the lack of support from a new wave of parents, guilty about the hours her work takes from family life, discouraged by a new and highly standardized curriculum, this dedicated teacher is paying an ever increasing "emotional toll" at work.

Alejandra remains conscientious and dedicated, but she now curbs her impulse to "play the parent" for children who receive limited guidance at home. She feels passionately that "teaching to the test" is a disservice to her children and expressed her indignation to the administrators who insist that she spend more time on test preparation and rote learning. The concerned teacher has yet to receive a response. These days, Alejandra is a bit more likely to "go with the flow," preferring to save her emotional energy for other more tractable causes. However, to counter her unfamiliar feelings of disenchantment, this veteran teacher actively seeks positive experiences. For example, a graduate class in educational technologies has recently captured her imagination. And Alejandra is cultivating stronger relationships with supportive colleagues. For the first time in her career, she has stopped working during her lunchbreak, taking time to chat, laugh, and commiserate with fellow teachers. By cutting back on her work hours, Alejandra made more time for unhurried conversations with her children and husband.

The veteran teacher views these efforts as evidence that she has become more "professional" and she knows that her emotional well-being has improved. Alejandra still feels the passion that drove her to become an educator but she sympathizes with the daunting challenges faced by rookie teachers. She reaches out to the newcomers, advising them to "pick your battles," and shushes her more jaundiced colleagues, who often share their bitterness over lunch in the teacher's lounge. "You have to strike the right balance in your life," Alejandra notes, "to stay emotionally healthy."

Alejandra's experience illustrates the broad array of emotions that color and vitalize working life – emotions such as awe and pride, admiration and guilt, indignation and sympathy. Table 1.2 documents those emotions and their apparent role in

Table 1.2   The roles played by emotions in Alejandra's work life

Emotion	Role in Alejandra's work life
Awe	Motivates Alejandra to teach children about the wonders of nature
Admiration	Assures her that her teaching is appreciated by parents
Camaraderie	Signals acceptance and support from colleagues
Disappointment	Indicates that Alejandra must adjust expectations for herself and her work
Guilt	Signals a need to rebalance work and family commitments
Hope	Helps her imagine a positive future; facilitates persistence
Indignation	Motivates Alejandra to protest against new testing regime
Pride	Indicates that professional aspirations are being met or exceeded
Sympathy	Prompts her to mentor new teachers

Alejandra's work. Her story also illustrates the crucial contribution of emotional *communication* as employees perform tasks, define relationships, enact organizational procedures and values, and negotiate the fluid boundaries that define their roles at work, home, and in society. In the case of this dedicated teacher, these contributions are manifested first at the individual level, in Alejandra's emotional characteristics and communicative dispositions. Her success in the seventh-grade classroom is due in part to the passion, enthusiasm, and hopeful outlook that she displays in her work. An emotionally competent employee, this teacher is skilled at assessing the feelings of others, recognizing, for example, the mixed feelings that her students may have developed toward science, as well as the frustration experienced by new teachers. Emotional communication plays an important role in Alejandra's relationships. Feelings of admiration, envy, camaraderie, and pride emerge from her interactions with peers, parents, family members, and students.

A third element of emotional communication is evident in the behaviors that school employees use to elicit and texture the emotions experienced by various audiences. We can see that Alejandra uses communication to cultivate awe in her students, curtail the toxic emotional displays of jaundiced peers, and express empathy for new teachers. A fourth contribution involves collective practices – the ways that employees cooperate to produce shared emotion. This is illustrated by the regular lunchtime gatherings of the teachers that create opportunities to vent feelings, offer support, and laugh. But it is in the school district's efforts to exercise power and control that a fifth contribution of emotional communication becomes obvious. Alejandra sees the new testing regimen imposed upon her and her students as an injustice, and she resists by expressing the emotion of indignation. But the school district apparently has no mechanism for responding to such expressions of "moral emotion," even when they are expressed by its most competent employees. A final role played by communication involves occupational and cultural discourses about the role of emotion in work. From these sources, Alejandra has learned the kinds of emotional behavior expected from "professional" teachers, supportive parents, and working mothers.

Good Work: Emotional Communication and Moral Meanings

Further reflection on Alejandra's experience illustrates a key theme of this book: that it is through the communication of emotion that organizations and employees enact workplace morality. It is a key influence on what organizations and individual employees consider to be worthy, just, right, and ultimately *good*, in the moral sense of the word. Alejandra illustrates this theme in several ways. First, her passion for teaching and awe of nature *motivate* her to be a good teacher, one that meets and exceeds the expectations of her employer and responds to the highest ideals of her profession. Second, the emotion of hope helps Alejandra to *envision a moral future*, one in which students share her own sense of wonder and experience the quality education that all students deserve. Third, emotions like indignation and guilt *signal moral concern*. They prompt Alejandra to protest against the new testing practices and to explore the misgiving she feels about her own family obligations. These efforts have the potential to restore justice and rebalance moral obligations. Finally, frustration and disenchantment make it obvious that the moral status quo is unsustainable. Alejandra seeks the camaraderie of her colleagues and broadens her search for positive emotional experiences. These activities are kinds of moral sense-making as she and her colleagues reassess their moral obligations, offer moral support, and redefine what constitutes "good work" at their school.

In short, Alejandra's emotions have been her moral guides, helping her do the right thing for her students, her school, her colleagues, her occupation, her family, and, ultimately, herself. This "do-gooding" was neither fully rational nor fully intentional. But it was definitely emotional. Feelings of guilt, though unwelcome (and way too familiar for parents who balance work outside and inside the home), prompted her to rebalance her commitments to family, students, and her employer. In the long run, this move could help Alejandra avoid career burnout and remain a vital teacher. That would be good for her students and her school. It was the feeling of sympathy that impelled Alejandra to offer new teachers advice and emotional protection, another case of doing the right thing in response to emotional cues. Finally, Alejandra had intended to fight the new curriculum by expressing her moral indignation. Having failed in this effort, she could have stewed in a justified feeling of bitterness. But this emotional setback was the very thing that drove her to develop closer bonds with colleagues. Supportive relationships are good in several senses of the word. They sustain the human spirit, fend off isolation, and, in this case, increase the chances that Alejandra's moral arguments about the testing regime will receive a larger audience. So, even as her emotional communication failed to persuade school district administrators, in a variety of ways Alejandra *did good*.

Survival of the Kindest?

In his thought-provoking book, *Born to be Good*, evolutionary psychologist Dachner Keltner (2009) revisits the Darwinian view of emotion, one that emphasizes the "survival value" of feelings as humankind evolved more complex social groupings. It takes little effort to imagine the modern workplace from a "survival of the fittest" evolutionary stance, with rewards accruing to those who are aggressive, selfish, and unbound by obligations to the collective. But Keltner reads Darwin in a different way, or, one might say, he simply emphasizes other aspects of Darwin's work. For Darwin argued in *The Descent of Man* (1871) that "social instincts" were signature advantages in evolutionary development, stronger than the instinct for self-preservation. Among these were caring for offspring, coming to the aid of group members, coordinating behavior through predictable social routines, the capacity for playfulness, and sympathy for other group members. From this perspective, emotions are a means by which these often admirable instincts are felt, expressed, recognized, and coordinated. Expressions of embarrassment (e.g., blushing) are an example, as they are recognition that a social code has been violated and signal deference to the larger social group that abides by them.

By living cooperatively in groups, animals (and humans) gained an evolutionary advantage. Darwin later articulated long lists of emotions which he presumed to have survival value, together with the means by which they were expressed (1872/1998). For example, guilt was thought to be expressed by poor eye contact and pained facial expressions. As Kelter explains, modern psychology has documented that many of these expressions are in fact "hard-wired" and universally recognized indicators of emotions. And emotion researchers, including communication researchers, are at work identifying the physiological and neurological signatures of these preprogrammed emotional states, such as affection or malice (e.g., Floyd, 2009). This research has stimulated much debate, with some scholars arguing that emotions can be explained with reference to just two underlying psychophysiologic continua: direction and intensity (Bolls, 2010). Intensity is the amount of arousal associated with a stimulus. Direction is the degree to which an organism responds to stimulus with a fight-or-flight response. For example, a stimulus may motivate us to flee if it is high on both the intensity and unpleasantness dimensions (that is, we are shocked by a boss's insulting comment), or to do nothing if it is low in intensity and moderately unpleasant (that is, a colleague grouses about our appearing at a meeting a few minutes late).

An alternative is the perspective of "discrete" emotions, which assumes that such work-related emotions as pride, jealousy, or indignation have unique psychophysiologic signatures (Nabi, 2010). One advantage of this approach is that it encourages us to think more concretely about the different kinds of emotions that people feel at work, the unique conditions that give rise to them, their different contributions to individual and organizational survival, and the means by which they are communicated. This discrete approach addresses two traditional problems in the literature on organizational emotion. First, researchers have too often lumped emotions into undifferentiated categories, such as job satisfaction or low morale. Second, where variety has been acknowledged, it concerns those emotions that are negatively, but not positively, valenced. Workers are often described with words such as *anger, envy, hostility, frustration, indignation, outrage, alienation, fear,* or *stress.* The positive emotions are harder to recognize and describe (but see Frederickson, 1998). However, one recent study of 850 of the "best" work experiences revealed that positive emotions were often reported and that they were typically associated with social dimensions of work (Lutgen-Sandvik, Riforgiate, and Fletcher, 2011).

What are some of those hard-to-name positive emotions? How about affection, calm, conviviality, awe, glee, admiration, delight, joy, cheerfulness, love, compassion, pride, astonishment, sympathy, or remorse? Feelings of confidence go a long way in the workplace, but then so does a dose of humility (Vera and Rodriguez-Lopez, 2004). Table 1.3 provides a longer list of these "prosocial" emotions and the kinds of interactions that yield them. As researchers and employees pay more attention to

Table 1.3 Selected prosocial emotions and workplace interactions that yield them

Emotion	Types of interaction
Awe (wonder, humility)	Encounters with inspiring, powerful, or mysterious forces
Admiration	Co-workers model desirable qualities and behaviors
Affection, liking	Interactions with similar or socially attractive peers
Calm	Tranquil or stable interactions or working conditions
Camaraderie	Experiences of solidarity or fellowship
Compassion	Observing distressed co-workers
Confidence/self assurances	Performing with coolness, ease, and certainty of purpose
Delight/joy/happiness	Pleasurable engagements with people or tasks
Excitement	Positively stimulating events or experiences
Embarrassment (mild)	Receiving gentle teasing or unexpected public recognition
Gratitude	Acts of altruism, kindness, or forgiveness
Hope	Optimistic communications; future-focused conversations
Mirth	Amusing or entertaining interactions
Pride	Recognition of self or group accomplishment
Remorse	Transgressions for which one wishes to atone

these prosocial feelings, it becomes clear that they do more than help us survive. They help us to thrive and flourish (Dutton and Heaphy, 2003). Indeed, for nearly a decade, scholars have argued that organizations need to appreciate and cultivate the naturally occurring positive behaviors that help humans, and their organizations, thrive in competitive environments (e.g., Luthans, 2002). Of course, we shouldn't be naive in doing so. Seemingly positive emotional practices can ultimately be unhelpful at work. False hope. Blind optimism. Misplaced confidence. These feelings can undermine relationships and lead to poor decisions. Nonetheless, organizational researchers are busy re-examining the "positive emotions" to better understand how they function at work.

Emotion-Guided, Interest-Sensitive Communication

I make these points not to argue that the role of emotion in complex organizations is limited to what Darwin observed long ago among the species of the Galapagos Islands (or as he carefully observed the family dog). Yet Darwin's thesis, filtered through modern psychological research, makes the point that social behavior, including workplace behavior, is in part instinctual and intuitive. It is *emotion guided*.

Emotion guided

By "emotion guided," I mean, first, that we are often unaware of how our emotions may have evolved to shape our communicative practices. Perhaps it is for perfectly sound evolutionary reasons that we feel fear in response to a particular facial expression or a tingle of warmth in the middle of a conversation with a sexually attractive co-worker. But we feel these things "automatically" and may respond instinctually (by leaving the room or offering a smile). Only later will we "make sense" of them in any mindful way (see Kellermann, 1992, and Planalp, 1999, for detailed discussion of issues related to automaticity).

Emotion guides employees in other ways. In Alejandra's case, feelings of hope prompted her efforts to expand the community of people who experienced the wonders of science. The gratitude of parents and the admiration of colleagues assured Alejandra that her work was advancing the interests of a larger community in which she was an important figure. In these cases, emotion had motivating effects on her behavior (see Weiner, 2006). In other cases, emotion directs our attention to something important, but previously unacknowledged. Feelings of guilt signaled that some of Alejandra's obligations were going unmet. She attended to them and made adjustments that helped herself and her family. Similarly, her growing sense of indignation signaled that something was "wrong" about her school's approach to education and prompted her to communicate her concerns. All of these examples demonstrate that emotion can guide us toward "good" behavior, toward practices that improve our well-being and that of the collective.

Of course, the emotions we consider to be negative, or antisocial, also have survival value. For example, feelings of anger can prompt aggressive "fight" responses, and those may be just what employees need when faced with competitors who are domineering, greedy, and unresponsive to cooperative behavior. Indeed, fearlessness is what allows employees to persist against the odds, whether they are soldiers battling a heavily armed enemy or whistleblowers taking on an unethical employer. In either case, the work is guided less by rational goals and more by emotional connections to comrades or important moral principles. And often it is the larger society that benefits, not the individual actor. So, if much of our emotional behavior at work turns out to be instinctual, it may also be the case that it is inherently useful, to us or the groups to which we belong.

Yet when we examine closely the ways in which emotion is communicated, particularly in the workplace, we see that it is much more than the subconscious "fuel" that drives us to behave in evolutionarily prescribed ways. Rather, it is a resource that organizations and individuals draw upon, often intentionally, to make work meaningful. It is a tool for defining and sustaining work relationships. It is a performance embedded in the work we do. Finally, emotion is a by-product of larger forces to which we are subjected when we work – the ways in which tasks are allocated and organized, organizational politics, external and internal missives, technologies of communication and surveillance, and the economic and industrial forces that impact our organizations. In all of these cases, emotion is produced through the symbolic behavior of people and organizations in pursuit of certain interests and goals. In this sense, emotional communication is not just emotion guided, it is also *interest sensitive*.

Interests and goals

What are these interests and goals? In this section I present only an abbreviated discussion of the ways in which emotional communication is used to advance the interests of organizations and employees. Further discussion is found in each of the subsequent chapters.

- *Productivity and task performance*: Organizations elicit feelings of trepidation or inspiration to motivate employees to meet productivity goals. Employees regulate and display emotions in performing certain tasks and advancing their career goals (see chapter 3).
- *Identity management*: Organizations construct emotional messages to create a favorable identity with external audiences. It is advantageous for a hospital to be perceived as compassionate or for a law firm to be passionate about defending its client's rights in court. Individual employees use emotion to protect their identities, by, for example, reacting with indignation to unfair criticism. They help sustain the identities of others by (for example) recognizing cues of embarrassment and coming to the rescue when a peer's identity is endangered by a social miscue.
- *Relationship maintenance:* Emotion is a social lubricant for work relationships. In disclosing their feelings, workers may intensify their connections. By editing feelings (such as envy or resentment), they maintain relationships that might otherwise be damaged. Some emotional displays, such as sheepish reactions to criticism, are acts of deference. They function to support, rather than contest, the existing system of power relations among co-workers. Beyond the level of interpersonal interactions, the larger organization also uses emotional communication to define and maintain relationships. It creates messages (e.g., stirring narratives about the founders), structures (the employee softball team), and rituals (e.g., sales rallies) to cement emotional bonds in the workforce. It creates norms that encourage "professionalism," a codeword that tells

21

employees to keep emotions at home where they are unlikely to upset the relational status quo. With customers, organizations maintain emotionally stable relationships by creating customer service departments, complaint handling systems, and rewards for customers who remain loyal, even through the emotional upheavals that accompany economic downturns.

- *Health promotion:* Emotional communication can be perceived as an indicator of well-being or of poor health. Positive employees are perceived to be well-adjusted. Those who seem too emotional are sometimes tagged as "mentally unstable" and encouraged to take time off. In some professions, such as nursing, supervisors may look for signs of emotional burnout and offer employees alternative work assignments. Organizations offer employees personal days, sabbaticals, or counseling services to keep them feeling "fresh" and ward off emotional exhaustion. The creation of emotionally fulfilling experiences, whether they be recognition programs, social events, or in-house yoga classes are part of the effort to promote feelings of well-being.

- *Moral signaling:* Some forms of emotional communication signal moral failure (see chapter 5). Organizations do this when they offer public expressions of remorse to customers or the public. Alternatively, they may try to cultivate feelings of moral outrage in the public if they feel that government regulations are unjustly limiting their opportunities for profit. When politicians decry the fate of the "heroic" small-business owners or criticize what they consider to be overreaching environmental "tree-huggers," they are trying to stoke the fires of moral outrage. When employees come to believe that their organization is violating accepted moral standards, they may respond by communicating indignation or even disgust. When expressed forcefully, these feelings may prompt the organization to treat employees with increased dignity, fairness, and justice. At the time of this writing, thousands of teachers are in the streets vociferously protesting efforts by the governor of Wisconsin to deny their right to form a union. Their outrage has captured the attention of the national media, but it remains to be seen if the governor will change course. Faced with an unresponsive management, employees such as these teachers sometimes feel compelled to seek moral redress in the courts or in the court of public opinion.

Emotionally Competent Employees

I have suggested thus far that communication research focuses on the symbolic aspects of emotion rather than its manifestations inside the individual. However, that is not entirely true. Both researchers and practitioners have been concerned with the communication competencies that employers bring to their jobs (see also chapter 2). Some of this interest traces back to the notion of emotional intelligence (EI), a concept popularized by psychologist Robert Goleman (1995). Goleman argued that traditional measures of intelligence failed to adequately capture importance aspects of human competence, including emotional ones. His conceptualization of EI included the capacities of recognizing and managing feelings in the self and others and using emotion for motivational purposes. Goleman's EI concept has been quite popular, largely because it resonates with intuitive notions about the interpersonal skills that make people likeable and successful. With the publication of Goleman's second book, *Working with Emotional Intelligence* (1998), corporate training and employee selection programs embraced EI and its various imitators as they sought to hire and develop those rare employees who could negotiate the tricky emotional terrain of the evolving workplace.

However, EI quickly came under fire from academics. They questioned the validity of EI measures, its reductionist and falsely rationalistic view of human feeling, and its failure to fully address the communicative dimensions of emotion (for an excellent critique, see Dougherty and Krone, 2002). Another criticism concerned the "selling" of EI as a quick fix for those seeking to improve their prospects for promotion in corporate settings (Fineman, 2000). As with so many corporate fads, EI was assumed to be a measurable and teachable competency – one that could be had by investing in the right employee selection tests and the correct training regimen. This approach arguably misses the richness of emotional experience and overestimates the degree to which feelings are cognitively accessible and under conscious control. Furthermore, Dougherty and Krone noted that moral and emotional sensibilities are different. It is entirely possible that employees high in EI may be more capable of manipulating others in an unethical manner. Finally, Fineman wondered why organizations assume that emotionally intelligent employees would use this capacity to advance organizational interests rather than those of employees or the larger society.

Despite these questions, it seems that emotional communication is an important part of interpersonal communication competence. Communication researchers provided evidence some time ago that a portion of the population exhibits an "affective orientation" toward interpersonal interactions (Booth-Butterfield and Booth Butterfield, 1994). That is, they were aware of their emotions and used emotion as information to guide their communication. In their extensive review of the research on the capacities of competent communicators, two of the field's pre-eminent researchers, Brian Spitzberg and William Cupach (2002), identified many emotional communication competencies. These include sensitivity to the emotions of others, ability to control emotion, and the capacity to express emotion. The interpersonal emotional competence scale (IECS) is a more recent development (Metts and Wood, 2008). This self-report scale measures the degree to which an individual *attends* to the emotions of self and others, *expresses* emotion, and co-*constructs* emotional meanings in interactions with other people. According to its developers, preliminary evidence suggests that scores on the IECS are correlated with scores on conversational knowledge and measures of social network integration. Although these studies were not conducted in work contexts, they do imply that employees who are competent in emotional communication will be more successful in conversation and in maintaining social networks, both of which are critical skills in many professions.

Finally, a key communication skill is the provision of emotional support (see also chapter 4). Team members and peers can be invaluable in helping co-workers feel better during emotionally troubled times, such as the aftermath of a poor performance evaluation or when family stresses interfere with work performance. And, of course, some jobs (e.g. social work, elementary school teaching, hospice care) may require skilled use of comforting messages. In a convincing body of research, communication scholar Brandt Burleson (e.g., Burleson, 2003) demonstrates that some communicators are more competent than others in providing social support. They use what Burleson and his colleagues call "person-centered" comforting messages. These messages explicitly recognize and legitimate emotions and help the distressed person communicate about them.

An employee who offered person-centered comforting might say things like, "I can see that you are feeling out of sorts today. It's OK if you need to express your frustration. I can see why you are upset. You are in a tough situation." Burleson (2008) notes that messages that minimize feelings ("It is no big deal"), emphasize the "silver lining," or co-opt the emotion ("I feel the exact same way!") are rated as less effective by message receivers. So it appears likely that some employees (those who tend to be person-centered) are better at providing emotional support than others (Burlseon, 2003). But Burleson's research suggests that most employees can be trained to use communication that makes other people feel better during times of distress. Given that disappointment and hurt are inevitable over the course of a career, such training would undoubtedly be useful.

Conclusion

This first chapter lays out the conceptual assumptions that guide me through the book. In particular, I have demonstrated that in the context of work, emotion can be productively considered a communicative phenomenon. The capacity to recognize and produce emotional displays seems to have evolved as a survival mechanism as animals, and then humans, adapted to life in complex organizations. But emotional communication is about more than organizational survival. I argued that the communication of "positive" feelings like hope and compassion help people flourish in organizational settings. The setting itself is important, as organizations provide unique opportunities for emotion to flow across networks, sustain or resist power relations, and create identities for various external audiences. Emotional communication performs other valuable functions, such as maintaining relationships and facilitating moral behavior. In a variety of ways, it can help employees and organizations to do good. I have depicted employees as creative negotiators of individual and organizational interests, but I have been careful to recognize that the sources and effects of emotion often lie beyond the control of individual employees. Emotions often guide us, but we don't always know where they are leading.

References

Aristotle (2000). *Nicomachean Ethics,* Book VIII. (R. Crisp, trans.). Cambridge: Cambridge University Press.

Bolls, P. D. (2010). Understanding emotion from a superordinate dimensional perspective: a productive way forward for communication processes and effects studies. *Communication Monographs*, 77: 146–53.

Booth-Butterfield, M., and Booth-Butterfield, S. (1994). The affective orientation to communication: conceptual and empirical distinctions. *Communication Quarterly*, 42; 331–44.

Bowe, J., Bowe, M., and Streeter, S. (2000). *Gig: Americans Talk about Their Jobs.* New York: Three Rivers Press.

Burleson, B. R. (2003). Emotional support skills. In J. O. Greene and B. R. Burleson (eds) , *Handbook of Communication and Social Interaction Skills.* Mahwah, NJ: Lawrence Erlbaum, pp. 551–94.

Burleson, B. R. (2008). What counts as effective emotional support: explorations of individual and situational differences. In M. Motley (ed.), *Studies in Applied Interpersonal Communication.* Los Angeles, CA: Sage, pp. 207–28.

Cicero, M. T. (2001). *Cicero on the Ideal Orator (De Oratore),* (J. M. May and J. Wisse, trans.). Oxford: Oxford University Press.

Darwin, C. (1871). *The Descent of Man.* London: John Murray.

Darwin, C. ([1872]1998). *The Expression of the Emotions in Man and Animals* (3rd edn). London: HarperCollins.

Dougherty, D., and Krone, K. J. (2002). Emotional intelligence as organizational communication: an examination of the construct. In W. B.

Gudykunst (ed.), *Communication Yearbook 26*. Newbury Park, CA: Sage, pp. 202–29.

Dutton, J. E., and Heaphy, E. (2003). Coming to life: the power of high quality connections at work. In K. Cameron. J. Dutton, and R. Quinn (eds), *Positive Organizational Scholarship*. San Francisco, CA: Barrett Koehler, pp. 779–814.

Fineman, S. (2000). Commodifying the emotionally intelligent. In S. Fineman (ed.), *Emotion in Organizations* (2nd edn). London, Sage, pp. 101–14.

Floyd, K. (2009). *Communicating Affection: Interpersonal Behavior and Social Context*. Cambridge: Cambridge University Press.

Frederickson, B. L. (1998). What good are positive emotions? *Review of General Psychology*, 2: 300–19

Frost, P. J. (2003). *Toxic Emotions at Work*. Cambridge, MA: Harvard Business School Press.

Goleman, D. (1995). *Emotional Intelligence: Why it Can Matter More than IQ*. New York: Bantam books.

Hochschild, A. R. (1979). Emotion work, feeling rules, and social structure. *American Journal of Sociology*, 85: 551–75.

Hochschild, A. (1983). *The Managed Heart*. Berkeley, CA: University of California Press.

Judge, T. A., Ilies, R., and Scott, B. R. (2005). Work–family conflict and emotions: effects at work and at home. *International Journal of Work, Organisation, and Emotion*, 1: 4–19.

Kellermann, K. (1992). Communication: inherently strategic and primarily automatic. *Communication Monographs*, 59: 288–300.

Keltner, D. (2009). *Born To Be Good*. New York: W.W. Norton & Company.

Krone, K. J. and Morgan, J. M. (2000). Emotion metaphors in management: the Chinese experience. In S. Fineman (ed.), *Emotion in Organizations* (2nd edn). London, Sage, pp. 83–100.

Lutgen-Sandvik, P., and Davenport-Sypher, B. (eds) (2009). *Destructive Organizational Communication: Processes, Consequences, and Constructive Ways of Organizing*. New York: Routledge, pp. 9–26.

Lutgen-Sandvik, P., Namie, G., and Namie, R. (2009). Workplace bullying: causes, consequences, and corrections. In P. Lutgen-Sandvik and B. Davenport-Sypher (eds), *Destructive Organizational Communication: Processes, Consequences, and Constructive Ways of Organizing*. New York: Routledge, pp. 27–52.

Lutgen-Sandvik, P., Riforgiate, S., and Fletcher, C. (2011). Work as a source of positive emotional experiences and the discourses informing positive assessement. *Western Journal of Communication*,75: 2–27.

Luthans, F. (2002). The need for and meaning of positive organizational behavior. *Journal of Organizational Behavior*, 23: 695–706.

Metts, S., and Wood, B. (2008). Interpersonal communication competence. In M. Motley (ed.), *Studies in Applied Interpersonal Communication*. Los Angeles, CA: Sage, pp. 267–86.

Miller, K., Considine, J., and Garner, J. (2007). "Let me tell you about my job": exploring the terrain of emotion in the workplace. *Management Communication Quarterly*, 20: 231–60.

Mumby, D. K., and Putnam, L. L. (1992). The politics of emotion: a feminist reading of bounded rationality. *Academy of Management Review*, 17: 465–86.

Nabi, R. L. (2010). The case for emphasizing discrete emotions in communication research. *Communication Monographs*, 77: 153–9.

Planalp, S. (1999). *Communicating Emotion: Social, Moral, and Political Processes*. Cambridge: Cambridge University Press.

Sandelands, L. E., and Boudens, C. J. (2000). Feeling at work. In S. Fineman (ed.), *Emotion in Organizations* (2nd edn). London: Sage, pp. 46–63.

Spitzburg, B. H., and Cupach, W. R (2002). Interpersonal skills. In M. L. Knapp and J. A. Daly (eds), *Handbook of Interpersonal Communication* (3rd edn), pp. 564–611.

Terkel, S. (1974) *Working: People Talk About What They Do All Day and How They Feel About What They Do*. NY: Pantheon/Random House.

Tracey, S. (2009). Managing burnout and moving toward employee engagement: Reinvigorating the study of stress at work. In P. Lutgen-Sandvik and B. Davenport-Sypher (eds), *Destructive Organizational Communication: Processes, Consequences, and Constructive Ways of Organizing*. New York: Routledge, pp. 9–26.

Tracy, S. J., and Tracy, K. (1998). Emotion labor at 911: a case study and theoretical critique. *Journal of Applied Communication Research*, 26: 390–411.

Van Maanen, J., and Kunda, G. (1989). Real feelings: emotional expressions and organization culture. In B. Staw and L. L. Cummings (eds), *Research in Organizational Behavior, Vol. 11*. Greenwich, CT: JAI Press, pp. 43–102.

Vera, D., and Rodriguez-Lopez, A. (2004). Strategic virtues: humility as a source of competitive advantage. *Organizational Dynamics*, 33(4): 393–408.

Waldron, V. (1994). Once more, *with feeling*: reconsidering the role of emotion in work. *Communication Yearbook* 17: 388–416.

Waldron V. (2009). Emotional tyranny at work: suppressing the moral emotions. In P. Lutgen-Sandvik and B. Davenport-Sypher (eds), *Destructive Organizational Communication: Processes, Consequences, and Constructive Ways of Organizing*. New York: Routledge, pp. 9-26.

Weiner, B. (2006). *Social Motivation, Justice, and the Moral Emotions: An Attributional Approach*. Mahwah, NJ: Lawrence Erlbaum Associates.

2

Communicating Emotion

Levels of Organization and Forms of Expression

Brownie, you're doin' a heck of a job!
> President George Bush, September, 2, 2005

In the aftermath of Hurricane Katrina, one of the largest natural disasters in United States history, Americans watched in horror as their televisions beamed pictures of the battered city of New Orleans. Marooned on sunbaked bridges and rooftops, surrounded by sewage-infested water, lacking food and medical supplies, the stranded citizens of this besieged city looked up in increasing desperation as helicopters passed them by and their health deteriorated. The unsettling stream of images continued for days and then weeks. It is fair to say that many citizens felt shame as it became obvious that storm victims were dying from inexplicable delays in the government's response to the emergency. It was against this backdrop that President George Bush stepped to a microphone and uttered the words reprinted above – an enthusiastic expression of confidence in Michael Brown, the leader of FEMA, the Federal Emergency Management Agency (White House, 2005). Some political commentators identify this moment as the tipping point in the president's precipitous slide in public opinion polls. Indeed, it appears that President Bush had misread the emotional mood of the American public. Although intended to boost the public's confidence in his staff, the president's message seemed to indicate that he was emotionally distant from the suffering of victims and the moral outrage felt by much of the citizenry.

29

This episode in recent American history illustrates an important theme of this chapter – that the way in which emotion is communicated by organizations and their representatives has potentially enormous consequences, inside and outside of the workplace. Emotional messages are scrutinized for their meaning, as various audiences form judgments about the organization's values, competency, and trustworthiness (see Keyton and Smith, 2009). Leaders are expected to communicate in ways that calm the fears of followers and instill confidence in times of crisis, but for some listeners, President's Bush's efforts to do so appeared inauthentic, given the "facts on the ground." The emotional message was inadequately adapted to the moment, a time when Americans might have expected an acknowledgment of their humiliation, expressions of anger at incompetent government executives, and perhaps the communication of remorse for the lives lost due to government incompetence. As is often the case with organizational leaders, the president's emotions were scrutinized by a large audience. The original message was shared across electronic media, its tone interpreted and reinterpreted by opinion leaders, and ultimately it shaped the public's assessment of the White House's emotional character. As is typical of organizational communication, the emotional residue of the Katrina press conference persists in the recollections of those who witnessed it. Its meaning is reinterpreted as witnesses tell the story and offer accounts (such as this one) of emotions that were felt at the time, the ones they expected to feel, and what they feel now.

Chapter 2 focuses on the many ways that emotion is communicated in the process of organizing. For our purposes, communication is the use of symbolic behavior to create meaning, coordinate behavior, define relationships, and achieve goals. Because emotion and communication are such integrated and overlapping aspects of social behavior, the length of this chapter could be infinite. Fortunately, excellent and comprehensive volumes have been published elsewhere (e.g., Andersen and Guerrero, 1998; Planalp, 1999; Keltner, 2009). So I will focus here on the communicative aspects of emotion that have particular significance in the workplace. In doing so, I will necessarily give short shrift to vast swathes of emotion research, such as that which examines the biological bases of emotion or the role of emotion in intimate relationships. The narrowed focus makes it possible to explore questions that are uniquely organizational. For example, in what ways might emotion be communicated across organizational networks? How do organizations produce emotion through their interactions with the larger society? Does the presence or absence of emotion signal something important about the health of an organization or a work relationship? In addressing such questions I consider, first, the various levels of organization at which emotional communication can be observed. Second, I address communication processes that are used to express, define, regulate, and sustain emotions in work settings.

Levels of Communication

A useful way to organize the landscape of emotional communication is to examine it at increasingly abstract levels of social organization – individual, relational, workgroup, organizational, occupational, societal, and global. Table 2.1 presents these levels, key communicative concerns for each level, and some of the questions that interest researchers and practitioners.

Individual

At the individual level, it is personality traits, personal skill, and bodily reactions to emotion that are paramount. As examples, consider that organizations might seek service workers with cheerful personalities, pilots who tend to remain calm under stressful conditions, or salespeople who show no physical signs of apprehension when making presentations or negotiating deals. A common assumption at this level is that the capacity to communicate emotion is an enduring personal disposition that can be "selected for" with various kinds of assessments (Fineman, 2000). Some of these measures replicate the emotional requirements of the job. For example, the communicative elements of a selection

Table 2.1 Emotional communication and levels of social organization

Level	Focal concepts	Sample questions
Individual	Traits, skills, biology	Is the employee emotionally competent? Are empathetic leaders more effective? What are the symptoms of emotional burnout?
Relational	Interaction patterns, relational messages, role requirements	How do coworkers describe their emotional bonds? Do members share fears with their leaders? Is emotion used to define power relations?
Workgroup	Networks, collective, moods, contagion	How does emotion spread across networks? Do emotional teams perform better or worse? What collective practices activate shared emotions?
Organization	Procedures, values/rewards, tasks, mechanisms, rituals, socialization practices, external messages	How is the expression of emotion regulated? Which emotions are new employees taught? How is emotion shared with external audiences? Which ceremonies are used to cultivate emotion? Is emotional communication integral to the service provided by the organization?
Occupation	Educational requirements, media portrayals, professional standards	In media depictions, which emotions are associated with this occupation? Which emotions are considered "unprofessional"? In what ways are emotional practices shared?
Society	National identity, social norms, economic values, gender roles	Are work and family separate emotional spheres? Is worker satisfaction an important social value? Does gender affect the allocation of emotion work? Are industries responsive to public fears?
Global	Cultural variations in definitions, values, and rules	Which workplace emotions are culturally unique? How are rules of expression similar or different? Are thinking and feeling dichotomized or placed on a continuum?

interview for a sales position may correspond quite closely to the sales process itself. Can the candidate maintain an enthusiastic demeanor? Does she remain positive in the face of criticism? Does he express negative feelings about past employers or sales assignments? In contrast, organizational theorists have questioned employers' considerable faith in paper and pencil assessments, with their assumed capacity to "tap" an employee's underlying emotional make-up (Dougherty and Krone, 2002; Nadesan, 1997). This individual-centered, test-centered approach certainly does reduce emotional communication to a few management-defined characteristics. And it can be criticized for underestimating the degree to which emotion is enacted in collaboration with others, rather than simply "released" from inside the individual. Ultimately, this conceptualization of emotion allows those who create and select measures of personality to determine the kinds of emotion that will be recognized and rewarded at work. Although it creates at least an illusion of predictability in the hiring process, that kind of control may impose unnecessary, and even harmful, limits on the kinds of emotional communication that can be enacted in the workplace.

Relational

At the relational level, emotion arises from the interactions of peers, leader and member, employee and customer. From this point of view, emotion is embedded in the role requirements and expectations that mold work relationships. But it is also enacted and sustained through discourse, the ways that employees talk (Fairhurst and Putnam, 2006). For example, the front-desk clerk at a car rental agency knows that she is *required* to engage customers in a pleasant manner; emotional intensity should be muted and never should she express irritation or annoyance. The customer expects roughly the same treatment. But it is through their communicative choices that clerk and customer enact these emotional requirements. The exchange begins with a cheerful, "How may I help you today?," rather than a surly "So, what do you want?" The customer typically matches the emotional tone, but if she reacts with an angry challenge, "Why did I have to wait so long?," the clerk may counter with a soothing response, "I am so sorry to keep you waiting." Faced with this conciliatory display of emotional moderation, the customer feels compelled to lower the emotional temperature, perhaps by making a sympathy plea: "I tell ya, it's been one hell of a day." "I hope I can make it better," the clerk offers with a smile. In this back-and-forth way, the parties dynamically shape emotional experiences while calibrating them to acceptable relational parameters.

In the interactions of leader and member, the emotion of fear may be the subject of relational negotiation. Oftentimes, the designation of leader brings with it greater license to manipulate emotions for legitimate organizational purposes. Thus it may be acceptable for a supervisor to use fear appeals to motivate members. She might do so by calling attention to scary circumstances ("The competition outsold us for the last three months") or by issuing bald threats ("If you don't work harder, heads will roll!"). Employees may not appreciate these fear-inducing messages, but they signal acceptance when they choose not to resist them. In some cases, they might even welcome them ("We were getting lazy and needed her to light a fire under us"). In contrast, less powerful members rarely attempt to induce fear in their leaders. Their restraint supports the emotional status quo. Knowledgeable about the organizational norms regulating emotions, veteran leaders and members *anticipate* emotional reactions and adjust their behavior accordingly. For fear of the consequences, they may choose not to "go over the head" of the boss (Kassing, 2007). To avoid feelings of regret, they may choose to accept a challenging assignment before it can be assigned to an up-and-coming, but status-hungry, co-worker. So, here again, emotion is intricately tied up in the communication that sustains work relationships.

Workgroup

For current purposes, the workgroup is considered a subcomponent of a larger organization – defined by a multiplicity of relational ties, common identity, and shared worked goals. Workgroups can be teams, task forces, or even whole departments. At this level, emotion is produced and magnified collectively, as in dyadic relationships. But the communicative contribution of any one member might be limited or hard to discern. Rather, it is the nature of the connections among members that is crucial. Consider that an angry outburst by one member of a department might be witnessed by only a few peers. Yet their reports of this emotional display are likely to be conveyed rapidly across the network as employees share the news and interpret its significance. The quality and magnitude of the emotion may change as it is filtered through brief conversations at the water cooler, forwarded across the office email system, and discussed when co-workers gather after work. Was the emotional display appropriate given the norms of the workgroup or an act of unprofessional malice? Was the agitated employee frustrated? Seething? Hysterical? How was this kind of emotional display dealt with in the past? Is it likely to happen again in the future? At the level of the workgroup, emotion buzzes across networks, surges like a wave, dissipates over time, and reconstitutes itself as workers share memories of the past. Initially, individual workers may experience only mild emotional reactions, a niggling sense of fear, a simmering feeling of indignation. But when certain events or group interactions stir these muted feelings, collective emotion can burst forth like a flame. Sasha recalled her own experience, in which whispered emotions finally ignited a revolt by members of her work team:

> I was working in a call center. The workers were always stressed because the queue was always backed up with at least eight calls waiting. The wait times were long and callers were always frustrated. The supervisors were supposed to help us out during busy times, but they just never did. As this kept happening I could tell that the employees were getting madder and we all started whispering about what to do. Finally, one time, we all just agreed to stand up and storm out, leaving the phone lines just blinking. This led to an intense stand-off in the break room with the supervisor angry and the employees expressing their feelings of frustration. Later there was a big meeting and that changed things for the better.

As this example suggests, some conditions make the spreading of emotion across networks, a phenomenon called *emotional contagion*, more likely (Wu and Hu, 2009). Emotions like pride or relief or resentment can lie just below the surface of conscious recognition, easily activated by the next rumor or perceived slight by management. An abusive manager may keep the group constantly "on edge" – on the verge of expressing resentment or fear. Or environmental conditions, such as a poor economy may leave workers feeling constant anxiety about the prospect of layoffs. In this case, a report of good economic news may prompt a surge of relief to spread, communicated by a series of smiling conversations or joyful whoops. On the other hand, constant low-level anxiety may result in a widespread feeling of gloom or collective sense of emotional exhaustion. Co-workers may surface these latent feelings in emotion talk ("Aren't you tired of these constant ups and downs"?) in a collaborative effort to ward off emotional exhaustion. However, repeated conversation can magnify disturbing emotional experiences and foster collective distress. Rafael, the leader of the community education department of a utility company, looked on in frustration as the operation was relocated under an unsympathetic administrator. With each administrative meeting, he became more frustrated by the bureaucratic inertia and outright hostility expressed toward his staff. As Rafael notes below, he and his colleagues made the emotional experience more acute by constantly reliving it.

> Every day at lunch we would tell stories of the new manager's incompetence and arrogance. How could they treat us so unfairly when they didn't even know what we did. Didn't these people get how much we had contributed and how hard we worked? We had these conversations at Happy Hour on Fridays and even during phone calls on the weekends. We were all so close, but every time I started to calm down, someone would start the whole thing over again and I would feel a burst of anger. After a few months of this my nerves were all jangled. I was bitter, and I just wanted to leave.

Interestingly, Rafael and his colleagues shared close emotional bonds, but these connections contributed to continuing flare-ups of agitation. For this workgroup, emotion is not a discrete experience communicated through messages, but something more like a mood that intensifies and relaxes in response to changing organizational circumstances and ongoing interactions.

Organizational

The communication practices of organizations are linked to emotion in myriad ways. For our purposes, organizations are defined as larger collectives comprised of interdependent individuals and workgroups united to achieve goals, such as the production of products or the delivery of services. Organizations create formal and informal structures as they attempt to impose order, improve coordination, and allocate power. Job requirements and promotion systems are just some of the structures that regulate emotional communication. They determine which kinds of emotions will be rewarded (e.g., pride in one's work) or punished (e.g., unenthusiastic responses to constructive criticism). Some work procedures provide highly specific instructions about emotional conduct, as when a front-desk clerk is required to smile at every customer. These emotional "display rules" are among the longest-studied aspects of organizational emotion (Hochschild, 1979, 1983). Less formal guidelines emerge without prompting from management. A familiar example would be a sign posted in an employee's workstation, reminding co-workers that "no whining" is allowed.

Communication scholars tend to view organizations not as static structures but as social entities with identities that are defined and sustained by ongoing discourses — the meanings created through talk, rituals, symbols, external campaigns, and the full range of symbolic behaviors (Fairhurst and Putnam, 2006). One kind of discourse is the organizational narrative, which often functions to define the emotional character of an organization (Frost, 2003). The author spent several years early in his career working on research and development for projects for a high-tech company that provided research services for the US government. He wrote this account in a personal letter about the experience.

The typical project slogs along for months at low priority. We spend lots of time doing "research" on the best techniques, trying to convince management to give us the resources we need. We argue a lot, take long lunches, and always end up at Happy Hour after work. But as the deadline for submitting the proposal approaches the pace gets frantic, management finally pays attention, and we work (literally) around the clock for as many as four days. Finally exhausted, the team puts some poor soul on an airplane to Washington D.C. where the proposal is delivered in person, hours before the deadline. Ever since I began working for *Anonymous Company*, I have heard tales of these last-minute heroics. The engineers talk about their frantic calculations, bleary-eyed mistakes, cat-napping in their offices, and the high speed run to the airport. The stories are told and retold with gusto, especially when new employees are in the vicinity.

These narratives were evidence of what employees called their "work hard, play hard" culture. The stories canonized employees who courageously sacrificed their health and family lives in the run-up to project completion and they fostered feelings of camaraderie on project teams. In their storytelling, team members signaled certain emotional requirements of life at *Anonymous Company:* whining was unacceptable; emotional ties to family members were less important than loyalty to colleagues; challenges should be accepted with humor; engineering work was physically exhausting but emotionally exhilarating. Of course, with a modicum of advanced planning, the projects could have been completed at a less frenzied pace. Mistakes could have been reduced. Overtime charges could have been curtailed. The strain on spouses and family members could have been minimized, and emotional exhaustion could have been avoided. Yet attempts to introduce these alternate practices might have radically changed the emotional bonds, the relational scaffolding that sustained the culture of this particular organization.

Emotion is managed through other internally and externally oriented organizational processes. Internally, members are socialized to emotional requirements through informal conversations with experienced employees and in formal training programs (Scott and Myers, 2005; also see chapter 3). Externally, public image advertising, crisis management efforts, and community outreach campaigns cultivate emotional responses in various audiences. For example, a petroleum products company might deploy a series of assuring advertisements to reduce public fears about toxic oil spills. A charity may use images of badly maimed children to evoke sympathy in prospective donors. The military cultivates feelings of patriotism, personal pride, and determination in advertising itself to potential recruits.

Occupational

Chapter 3 considers, in detail, occupations for which emotional communication is an important component, including hospice workers, stand-up comedians, athletic coaches, and soldiers. An employee's occupation offers a professional identity that transcends any given organization (Lammers and Garcia, 2009). As observed in a recent study of teachers and managers in the UK, occupational training may be more important in shaping communication than organization-specific norms (Coupland, Brown, Daniels, and Humphreys, 2008). In interviews, this tendency was observed in reference to "speakable emotions," the feelings that employees acknowledged and legitimated as part of their profession. For example, managers tended to downgrade emotions, denying or minimizing experiences of anxiety or depression and labeling such feelings as unprofessional. In contrast, teachers tended to recognize emotion as a legitimate part of the work they performed; they appeared to be more at ease with the emotional performances they encountered at work. One male teacher described his emotional response to an unruly class: "after the initial shouting and screaming and stamping my feet I've just got on and prepared a load of work for them" (Coupland et al., 2008: 336).

Societal

Communication at work is in part a function of larger societal norms (Nadesan, 1997). One example involves the ways in which male and female leaders are expected to communicate emotion. The issue came to the fore in the 2008 US presidential campaign, when Hilary Clinton, a prominent female candidate, shed tears during an apparently heartfelt visit with her supporters in New Hampshire. This emotional display touched off a round of speculation by political commentators, some of whom suspected that Clinton was trying to humanize her personality, which was perceived to be too "emotionally chilly" for an American female leader. An illustrative article was printed in the *Washington Times*, which wondered if Clinton had won the "crying game" (Bellantoni, 2008). The article reported that Clinton rode her "comeback cry" to a surprise victory in the primary election. In the article, a Clinton backer argued that her tears revealed natural warmth and allowed her to connect with female followers. Her campaign chairman praised the candidate for showing compassion, but critics questioned her emotional authenticity, apparently because she had been insufficiently warm (for a female?) in previous appearances. The coverage revealed the way that the communication practices of female leaders (in particular) are filtered through cultural expectations about emotionality. Media observers raised questions about the emotional behavior of a potential president. But they also questioned whether her behavior was appropriate for a female. Clinton herself acknowledged the challenge for female leaders:

> Maybe it's a little more challenging for a woman in this position because, obviously, we know what people will say, but maybe I have liberated us to actually let women be human beings in public life. (Bellantoni, 2008: A01)

Global

Finally, given that societies are defined by different linguistic, religious, and social traditions, it is not surprising that emotional communication varies globally. In their analyses of Chinese emotionality, organizational communication scholars Kathleen Krone and Jayne Morgan (2000) contrasted the thought–feeling continuity of the Chinese with the mind–heart dichotomy commonly found in Western cultures. Chinese children develop an identity that emphasizes their role within a well-defined network of familial and cultural relationships. In contrast, US children are generally taught to define themselves as autonomous individuals, separated from others by distinct personal boundaries. In a study of 48 Chinese executives, Krone and Morgan observed that these differences in identity extended to workplace experiences of emotion. In particular, they examined the kinds of metaphors that emerged when the managers described pleasant and unpleasant emotional experiences. Whereas US managers tend to describe unpleasant emotion as a temporary state that must be captured within the "container" of the person, a "homeostasis" metaphor seemed to capture the reports of Chinese managers. They described a process of cooling and calming as critical in restoring good relations with others and they emphasized the restoration of inner harmony. Emotion was also a source of learning about one's role in the culture of the organization, as suggested by one manager's instruction to an employee who was the target of an emotional outburst: "This is a lesson of blood. You should learn it by heart and improve yourself" (p. 93).

All of this reminds us that communication of, or about, emotion will vary considerably as employees travel across international and cultural borders. Western employees may be puzzled by statements such as "thoughts are felt in the heart" (Young, 1994: 118), a Chinese expression that reflects the seamless continuity of heart and mind. In Japan, an emotional experience described as "sweet dependence" (Morsback and Tyler, 1986) will be unfamiliar to travelers from the US, who are often taught that feelings of dependency should be left behind as people mature. Eastern employees from collectivist cultures may need assistance in understanding the way that pride is frequently expressed in the US with regards to individual, as well as collective, accomplishment.

Processes of Emotional Communication

Although emotional responses are often the intended outcome of strategic messages created by organizations and their members, feelings are connected to communication in a variety of other ways. Emotion is often expressed unintentionally at work, as when an embarrassed gasp escapes the lips of an employee who has just witnessed a co-worker's social gaffe. And, of course, the intended meaning of a message may not be that which is constructed by its audience. Much to their consternation, the excuses employees offer for tardiness or poor performance are often met by a supervisor's indifference or scorn, not the sympathy that was intended. To make things more complicated, emotion is often elicited not by some message, or string of messages, but instead by exposure to ambiguous non-verbal cues, participation in organizational rituals, or acceptance of work identities. In other words, emotion is often an unconscious by-product of other communication processes. My intention in this section is to chronicle some of these varied forms of communicative experience, starting with those grounded in concrete non-verbal aspects of behavior and moving to progressively more abstract and complicated forms of expression.

Non-verbal cues

Communication is partly a matter of recognizing and interpreting the non-verbal cues associated with various feelings (Burgoon and Le Poire, 1999; Planalp, 1999). Many of these cues are familiar. Some seem to be universal, apparently grounded in the biological hardware shared by humankind (for an interesting recent review, see Keltner, 2009). For example, most employees would recognize the menacing tone of voice that means a supervisor is angry, the flush of skin color that signals a co-worker's embarrassment, or the facial expressions that suggest a client is happy with a service. Sarcasm is another widely recognized example, communicated largely through tone of voice. In workgroups, it sends a powerful message about who is in charge. Jana worked in the office of a design engineering firm. She described how one volatile manager responded to a secretary's modest mistake (she apparently waited too long before passing on a phone message). When the employee offered to make up for the mistake by contacting the caller, he responded in a biting tone "Oh, what a generous offer ... Did you think I should just waste more time picking up the ball that you just booted around? Nice job [name]. You are a real pro." Julianna reports that she and her co-workers looked on in horror as their colleague was humiliated. The incident has had a "chilling effect" on the office. She lives in fear of making a similar mistake and receiving similar treatment.

Although much of this non-verbal communication appears instinctual, there is much to be learned. Some non-verbal cues are quite ambiguous, so the employee must interpret them in terms of organizational and relational norms. They use cues and context to make judgments about the internal states of the emoter (see Weiner, 2006, for a detailed description of attributional approaches to emotion). Take the leader who habitually (but insincerely) smiles when chatting with team leaders, even when he or she plans to reject their urgent requests for additional resources. The instinctual response to smiling behavior is to interpret it as a sign of liking, cooperation, or even safety. However, over time employees come to recognize the leader's pattern of non-verbal behavior as a kind of facade, a way to avoid conflict while leaving everyone with a pleasant feeling. In this way, a layer of social complexity is added to biologically grounded communication mechanisms. Employees learn to question their instinctual emotional responses to non-verbal cues and to make social judgments about them.

Table 2.2 provides additional examples of organizational contexts, non-verbal cues, and the kinds of questions that employees might ask themselves or others as they interpret them. Even when cues have, by default, a particular cross-contextual meaning, a first consideration is the context in which the cue is perceived. For example, the aversion of eye gaze is in biological terms a sign of meekness, a signal that the communicator is intimidated by a powerful rival or at least willing to submit to the existing social order (Keltner, 2009). But its meaning may be ambiguous in a

Table 2.2 Selected work contexts, cues, and interpretative considerations

Context	Cues	Interpretative concerns
Job interview	Poor eye contact	Ambiguity: which emotion applies?
Team meeting	Angry vocal tone	Appropriateness: are norms violated?
Resource request	Smile, nod	Authenticity: is the support authentic?
Informal chat	Intrusive touch	Consistency: has a pattern developed?

job interview. Is the candidate anxious? Lacking in confidence? Distracted? Other interpretive concerns become relevant when we are confronted with non-verbal cues:

Appropriateness: does the use of an angry tone of voice conform to emotional norms of the workgroup?

Authenticity: does the appearance created by smiling and head-nodding comport with the "real feelings" of the communicator?

Consistency: is a co-worker's touch incidental or is an alarming pattern developing over repeated instances of seemingly inappropriate touch?

In addition to interpreting non-verbal cues, emotional communication involves their production. Again, some of this behavior seems to be biologically preprogrammed. Skilled poker players come to recognize the subtle, "automatic" signs of pleasure that may signal the opponent has drawn a good hand. Yet much of what Hochschild (1983) identified as emotional labor involves the *production* of non-verbal cues or the capacity to mask those that might otherwise be recognizable by an audience. Restaurant servers learn to disguise their disgust with customers who offer insultingly low tips. The emotion is hidden by the fabricated smile and the cheerful voice. Courtroom lawyers learn to tilt their head in a display of deference to the judge and police officers display a poker-faced calm during potentially risky encounters with erratically driving motorists. In these ways, emotional communication involves recognition, interpretation, and production of job-related cues.

Words and language

The discourse of organizations is peppered with the language of emotion. Emotion words are often used to label co-workers. Table 2.3 provides a list of emotional labels found in a brief and random tour of recent postings to work-related Internet sites such as officepolitics.com and jobschmob.com. Hardly inclusive, the list conveys the many ways that language links emotion with work identity. In this list, the language of "negative" emotion seems more articulated than that of positive emotion, an observation that may indicate organizational life offers more variations of unpleasant feeling. Another explanation is more likely. The abundance of negative emotion words may simply reflect the preference of employees to vent negative feelings in anonymous posts to the

Table 2.3 Selected emotional words and phrases from work-related Internet sites

angry	awe inspiring	bitchy
calm/calming	cheery	clammy
cold/cold feet	confident	coward
dead	deer in the headlights	depressing
distant	downer	draining
drama queen	emotional basket case	emotional suction cup
emotional train wreck	excited	explosive
fearless	fiery	fun
happy as a clam	hard-hearted	heartless
high maintenance	hostile	hot headed
humbled	hyper-enthusiastic	joy to have around
mellow	misty-eyed	moody
mopey	needy	negative
on edge	out of control	over/undercarbonated
passionate	pissy	positive
proud as a peacock	radiant	scaredy cat
sensitive	soothing	spineless
stable	stressed	thick/thin-skinned
touchy	unprofessional	uplifting
volatile	volcanic	wacked-out emotional
weepy	wet blanket	

Internet. Perhaps positive emotions can be shared more safely in the workplace.

Emotion words also give clues about the personal qualities that are valued by fellow employees. Emotional predictability is well represented by terms like *stability*, *explosiveness*, and *volatility*. But emotional (over)sensitivity is another common theme, represented by terms like *bitchy*, *pouty*, *touchy*, and *thin-skinned*. A border patrol officer described the phrases that were used by his (all-male) peers to tease a co-worker who seemed moody and overly sensitive. "Would you like to be tucked in for a nap?" "Do you need to sniffle in my hanky?" "Do you want me to hold you and put a nipple on your beer?" At other times, language is used to link emotion with a temporary loss of sanity or personal control. A co-worker is labeled a "basket case" or a "train wreck." A worker described a brief fit of uncontrolled anger this way: "I just went off on him. I just couldn't stop myself." Some of the terms in table 3.3 describe endearing emotional dispositions (kind-hearted, compassionate, calming), but some co-workers apparently are guilty of intentionally inflicting emotional hurt. They are said to be vicious, ugly, or hostile. In contrast, some people are credited with altering the collective mood of the workgroup, making it fun, uplifting, or depressing. Finally, it is obvious that some terms, such as "bitchy" or "grumpy bastard," are gendered, a reflection of larger societal biases (see above).

Slogans are catchphrases designed to capture the essence of an organization. In some cases that essence is emotional. Slogans define the organization for its external audiences. On a billboard in my city, one hospital boasts about its "culture of caring" and an insurance company pledges to "stand by our customers every step of the way" in the aftermath of a car accident. On local television, a legal firm touts its ferocity in "fighting for clients" that have been charged with DUI or minor legal offenses. These messages market emotional assurance to clients who may, some day, experience serious emotional distress. They suggest that the organization itself is a site of emotional stability.

Management often crafts internally directed slogans with emotional themes. At an engineering firm I worked for, employees were instructed by management to "show no fear" and "take no prisoners" as they competed against foreign business rivals. A local social services agency calls itself Children at Hope, invoking this positive emotion as an alternative to the typical "children at risk" nomenclature. In another example of emotional self-labeling, those who serve in one branch of the US military frequently hear the message "proud to be a marine." Employees at Carnegie Mellon University were explicitly encouraged to make an emotional investment in their jobs. Their slogan? "My heart is in the work."

This identity-making communication emerges informally as well, as employees come to define the emotional textures of their work environment. Researchers of emotion sometimes listen for the metaphors that emerge as employees describe the role of emotion in their occupations (e.g., Krone and Morgan, 2000). Metaphors are forms of speech that explain an unfamiliar experience by referencing a more familiar phenomenon. Some emotion metaphors are obvious in our everyday interaction. People struggle with anger (as they would an enemy), fall in love (as if it were an abyss), and become insanely jealous or love sick (as if emotion were a mental or physical disease). In the workplace, metaphors make it possible for employees to describe feelings that have no easy equivalent in private life: the emotional "kick" received from a truly satisfying form of work; the creative spark ignited by the interactions of a diversely talented team; the angst of observing long-time colleagues lose their jobs.

Metaphors bring to the foreground certain aspects of complex experiences, even as they de-emphasize others. At my university, employees have experienced several years of budget cuts, nearly constant reorganization, and staff terminations. Those who lost colleagues during this time describe themselves as "emotionally devastated" by the waves of bad news, much like victims of a storm. They feel "numb," "shock," "doomed," and "drained," and some think administrators are out of touch with the emotional consequences of their actions. However, organizational subcultures are typically fragmented and emotional responses are rarely uniform (Martin, 1992). Co-workers use competing metaphors to reflect their local circumstances and offer alternative interpretations of organizational events. Indeed, some university employees have invoked alternate metaphors, such as "riding out the storm," "survival of the fittest," or "cutting out the dead wood." For them, the recent budget-cutting created feelings of relief, renewed hope for those who remain, safety from future cuts, and a sense of self-satisfaction that comes from surviving the bad times. Still other metaphors have emerged to interpret this unsettled period in our organization's history. One administrator, nonplussed by constantly changing budget projections and the wildly unpredictable behavior of her bosses, threw up her hands and described the situation as a "theater of the absurd." In other words, emotion and reason were no longer bound together. Employees might as well "enjoy the show."

Other metaphors emerge in my own observations of various organizations. Employees at a state agency described their organization as "under siege" and in "constant battle" with the governor's office. They described feelings of nervous anticipation, contempt for the enemy, fear of the future, and resentment at the unfairness of their situation. Employees at a call center, faced with demanding quotas, described the job as a "pressure cooker." High-school teachers expressed disgust as they were forced to act as "babysitters" for petulant students who had no interest in learning. Social workers lamented that they could provide only an "emotional band aid" to children who were stuck in dysfunctional family situations. Factory workers used the term "family" to describe the close emotional bonds they had developed with peers. An engineer decried the limited emotional repertoire of her co-workers, who spent much of their time boasting about the victories of their fantasy league sports teams and criticizing the latest edition of their favorite computer games. "Automatons" and "emotional midgets" were labels she suggested for these peers. All of these examples demonstrate that employees use an inventive and nuanced language to define the emotional textures of their organizations and their work relationships.

Tactics

If we imagine a strategy to be the abstract approach a communicator adopts in pursuing a goal, tactics are the more concrete communicative practices used to implement the strategy. They are created from the non-verbal cues and language practices discussed above. For example, imagine an employee with the goal of building a collegial relationship with a new boss. He or she may settle on the general approach of flattery. But how is flattery accomplished? The tactics of the flatterer include offering compliments, muting criticism, publicly defending the boss from the attacks of other employees, and frequently expressing agreement. These tactics all involve verbal ("Wow! That's a nice tie") and non-verbal (smiles; eye gaze) communicative elements. Of course, the language of tactics and strategies invokes a certain "war games" metaphor in which participants are mindful, calculating, and competitive. Communication, especially emotional communication, often exhibits none of these qualities (see Planalp, 1999, for a review of the theoretical issues). Nonetheless, as I have argued elsewhere (Waldron, 2009), organizations and individual employees frequently link communication and emotion in a mindful effort to advance their goals – to create identities, regulate relationships, complete tasks, and manage health and well-being.

As table 2.4 suggests, emotional communication tactics come in a variety of forms. The table provides illustrative examples of four tactic types. In some cases communication is used to elicit emotion in others. When service organizations urge employees to not just serve, but "delight" a customer, they are endorsing the use of emotional elicitation tactics. Employees elicit feelings of delight by exceeding expectations, not just meeting them (which presumably would elicit the lesser emotional response of satisfaction). One can imagine the escalating communicative demands on employees as customers continue to raise their expectations. What emotional experience could be more positive than delight? A chain of restaurants in the San Francisco area gives us a hint. Its name? *Pizza Orgasmica.*

Tactical efforts to elicit emotion are easily observed in most

Table 2.4 Emotional communication tactics with illustrative examples

Emotional eliciting	*Emotional regulating*
Delighting a customer	Toning down expressions of joy
Intentionally embarrassing a colleague	Ignoring expressions of contempt
Publicly humiliating a whistleblower	Stopping emotional gossip
"Charging up" an athletic team	Teaching "controlled aggression"
Invoking sympathy from the public	Allowing the boss to "cool down"
Offering hope to a patient	Refusing to share emotion-laden rumors
"Guilting" an employee into staying late	Discounting expressions of alarm
	Nurturing bitterness
Emotion labeling	*Emotional transforming*
Suggesting that an organization is "saddened" by its mistakes	Bolstering courage in the face of fear
Self-identifying as a positive person	Seeking vengeance as an alternative to anger
Denouncing co-workers as whiners	Humanizing as a way to transform bitterness into compassion
Describing a team as excited about a project	Articulating hope in response to a dispiriting tragedy
Acknowledging grief over loss of a patient	Offering inspiration to a fearful employee
Noting that workforce is "on edge"	Using humor to replace anxiety with relief
Calling a worker's behavior "inspiring"	Banishing guilt and encouraging resolve
Describing yourself as "angry" instead of "fearful"	Reframing feelings of consternation as concern

workplaces. The jealous colleague who intentionally embarrasses a star performer is extracting retribution. By eliciting embarrassment, the attacker exercises relational power and undermines the co-worker's competence. Organizations may use emotion to discourage whistleblowers or "complainers." At my university, departments that disagree with the administration are sometimes "called out" in speeches and public statements, presumably with the intention of humiliating them into silence. Organizations try to cow whistleblowers by releasing damaging anecdotes (collected from colleagues or supervisors) to the public. Emotional appeals are among the most familiar tools of persuasion, and organizations frequently use fear or sympathy appeals to curry favor with the public or defend their images during a crisis. When accused of wrongdoing, a company might elicit sympathy by claiming to be victimized by rogue employees, vicious public-interest groups, or meddling government agencies. In the spring and summer of 2010, a large oil spill in the Gulf of Mexico had oil industry executives pointing fingers at allegedly unscrupulous contractors. Oil industry supporters were blaming government regulations that "forced them" to drill in deep waters far off the coast, where the consequences of equipment failure are magnified. Opinion polls suggest that the public remains unsympathetic in the face of these claims.

The tactical use of emotional labels allows communicators to take advantage of societal or organizational biases regarding emotion. Given that emotions are complex and ambiguous, labeling allows the communicator to help others make sense of emotional displays. Is a co-worker "whiney" or simply giving voice to justifiable concerns? Is the work team stressed out by a demanding new project or just excited by the opportunity to try something new? Is it OK for a hospice worker to express grief over the loss of a long-time patient, or does that form of feeling suggest too much personal involvement? What would it mean if a job applicant was realistic rather than totally enthusiastic in his or her assessment of the performance? Is it OK for doctors to describe feelings of remorse after a failed operation, or would that label make them vulnerable in a malpractice lawsuit?

Unlike the first two tactic types, emotional regulation tactics neither create new emotion nor define those that are observed. Rather, they start with the assumption that emotion is being experienced but attempt to alter its qualities. When a co-worker shouts "Tone it down!" to bickering peers, he or she is regulating the intensity of emotional expression, perhaps in the hope that the team will be spared the consequences of unbridled emotion displays. Workers sometimes try not to look "too joyful" upon receiving a promotion so as not to create the impression of boasting (Waldron and Krone, 1991). The supervisor who attempts to "damp down" the fears of a workforce and the coach who "revs up" a team are using communication to regulate emotional experiences. When employees refuse to pass on a wild rumor, engage in group bitch sessions, or propagate an emailed diatribe, they work the emotional throttle of an organization's communication network. These tactics may dampen emotion and inhibit the process of emotional contagion (Maslach, 1982). Existing emotions also can be magnified intentionally, as when through repeated conversations employees nurture grudges, build confidence, or inflame emotional wounds.

Emotion regulation is an important element of the work performed in crisis situations by firefighters, 911 operators, and other emergency responders. Firefighters are socialized to use controlled aggression when working a dangerous structural fire (Scott and Myers, 2005). The work requires courage and determined effort, but excessive aggression results in risky behavior and foolish mistakes. Faced with distraught members of the public and their own feelings of distress, crises workers must perform what Tracy and Tracy (1998) call "double-faced" emotion management. Essentially, they regulate the emotion of others by limiting their own emotional responses. Yet another tactic is compartmentalizing or "buffering" emotions (Ashford and Humphrey, 1995). One compartmentalization strategy is to direct a co-worker's attention to less emotional aspects of the job: "You can't do anything about that mistake now. Focus on what you can do." In a similar way, emergency responders regulate grief when they focus on helping accident victims who can be saved while directing attention away from those who have died at the scene.

Finally, transformative tactics change existing emotions into new ones. The familiar slogan "don't get angry, get even" encourages workers to transform anger into the emotional satisfaction that sometimes comes with revenge. On the other hand, "rehumanizing" an offending party, by exploring their motives and emotions, sometimes allows co-workers to release feelings of bitterness and replace them with compassion (Waldron and Kelley, 2008). The expression of remorse by a transgressor often transforms the negative feelings of the offended party. In other versions of transformation, an employee who fears public speaking may be emboldened by positive feedback from colleagues in the audience. Discouraged employees may find feelings of inspiration when exposed to credible stories of triumph and success. In human service work, the tendency to feel emotionally burned-out may be replaced by feelings of emotional competence when workers learn to "feel for" clients rather than "feel with" them (Miller and Koesten, 2008). A final example of transformation involves humor. A well-timed quip can change feelings of anxiety or annoyance into hilarity and relief. However, a poorly selected joke can have the opposite effect, changing the mood of colleagues from comfortable camaraderie to acute embarrassment.

Interaction sequences

When communication is viewed through a tactical lens, the focus is on a single communicator and his or her message. In contrast, an interactive view assumes that communication shapes emotion over a series of conversational turns (Fairhust and Putnam, 2006). Each utterance is responsive to the last, even as it moves the conversation forward and contributes to the flow of meaning. From this vantage point, emotional experiences are constructed through the cooperative contributions of co-workers and team members, although the unfolding discourse may be fragmented, unintentional, and "messy." Organization members may not be consciously aware of the ways in which their exchanges are altering emotions and they often experience unintended emotional consequences. Interaction sequences may be ritualized, as might be the case when a group of teachers begins each day with coffee and mutual venting about the administration or problematic parents. However, emotional interactions are also spontaneous and inventive. For example, a co-worker may be "unusually smiley," prompting his peers to pepper him with a series of semi-random questions about the reasons for his good humor. Did he have a successful date the night before? Win the office betting pool? Is he receiving a raise? His coy unwillingness to disclose may then touch off a round of pleading (*"Come on*, you can share your secret with us, your trusted co-workers . . .") or good-natured "guilting" ("If *we* had good news it would be shared with everyone!").

Interactive emotional communication may serve goals similar to those associated with tactics (see above), such as managing relationships or sustaining identities. However, the communicative possibilities are enriched by the contributions of multiple parties, pressure to reciprocate, use of temporal cues ("Why is he taking so long to answer my question?"), and the capacity to alter emotions with each conversational turn. Emotional modification comes in the form of feedback, follow-up questions, and metacommunication (messages about the ongoing processes of communication). A response of this kind might be: "You sounded agitated when I asked you that question. Am I getting on your nerves?" Discourse-based communication researchers have provided excellent analyses of the forms of interaction (e.g., questioning) that organizational members use to sustain their "institutional identities." An example would be the question-and-answer routines that sustain the emotional tone and power of the relationships among judges and other courtroom participants (Tracy, 2009).

Interactive discourse is the means by which organizational reality is reflected, organized, and enacted (Fairhurst and Putnam, 2006). Here I present a selection of the kinds of interaction patterns that shape emotional experiences at work. *Emotion-reflecting* sequences reify the emotions that are thought by members to define the essence of an organization. I observed a conversation between two actors about the reactions of a third performer to the news that he would not be selected for a part. As Actor 1 notes, hysterical emotion displays are not part of the troupe's emotional repertoire.

Actor 1: His face went white and his eyes bugged out. I thought he would faint, but he started to moan in a loud voice. Then he shouted some bad, bad words.
Actor 2: He got crazy?
Actor 1: Yes, he got hysterical. We don't *do* hysterical here.

Emotion sharpening

These sequences add zest and spice to the menu of organizational experiences, often in response to language which flattens, dulls, or abstracts emotional events. I heard two university employees talking after a recent layoff. Employee B's response encourages the pair to substitute more specific emotional labels ("outrageous") and physical reactions ("makes me feel sick") for the initially abstracted, "it sucks" description.

Employee A: It kind of sucks that [person x] got let go after all of these years.
Employee B: It more than sucks. It is *outrageous*! She worked here for like 15 years and she was one of our best employees. It actually makes me feel sick to my stomach.
Employee A: Me too. I am worried. Who's next? It scares me.

Emotion-*normalizing* sequences are used to reframe what initially appears to be extreme or unusual emotion as typical or expected. This kind of behavior was observed in a recent study of the socialization of firefighters (Scott and Myers, 2005) who must adjust to the extreme emotional reactions of accident victims and relatives. Another example comes from my own experience: When my daughter played high-school basketball I watched with some consternation as her coach stomped around the sidelines in wild-eyed anger, screamed the "F bomb," and occasionally hurled chairs to make his point with the referees. He accused his players of being cowardly "pussies." As concerned parents, my wife and I scheduled a meeting with the athletic director (AD) and the coach to express concerns about what (to us) appeared to be unusual and irresponsible expressions of emotion. The AD normalized the coach's emotional displays by contrasting the modern high school with those of the past, suggesting that other parents supported the emotional displays, linking emotion to the organizational goal of "winning," and suggesting that the coach had intended to use a less offensive "F word."

AD: What seems to be the problem?

Parent: We have some concerns about coach's language at practice and in the games. We are wondering if his emotions are getting the best of him sometimes.

AD: Can you give an example?

Parent: The use of the "F word" would be one example; the screaming and kicking the chairs on to the court. Do we want the kids to model that behavior?

AD: Well, you know it's not like when we went to school ... These kids' parents want them to get scholarships and they want an aggressive coach like other schools have. Some of these kids need discipline. They expect to be yelled at. That's why we brought coach here. He knows how to win.

Parent: Is screaming the "F word" really appropriate behavior for a high-school coach?

AD: Well, I think the coach said "friggin," not the other word. Or at least that is what he meant. Right, coach?

Emotion uncovering

These sequences involve the disclosure or discovery of emotion that might otherwise be hidden from view. It can take the form of questions like, "Are you OK? I noticed you haven't been saying much at lunch," and confessional responses of the type, "Well, I am feeling disgusted with my teenager, but it's not the kind of thing I share with the team." *Emotion-disciplining* sequences correct emotional mistakes. Upon being questioned in recent government hearings about apparently unsavory business practices, the CEOs of major investment firms repeatedly professed that their behavior was legal, but "nothing to be proud of." *Emotional-deepening* sequences assure that fellow employees experience an emotion fully. I once unintentionally offended a colleague with an off-handed comment about her research. I could tell immediately that she was hurt and I offered a quick apology. She responded with silence and then an awkward ending to the conversation ("OK, thanks for dropping by"). I returned to my office, ruminating over the event, and feeling a deepening sense of remorse. The next day, I visited her again, expressing that I felt "really badly" about my remark and couldn't stop thinking about it. She smiled and thanked me. "I needed some time to feel angry," she said, "and I was hoping you were feeling bad too." In these ways, interaction sequences allow emotions to simmer, marinate, and penetrate the consciousness of organizational actors.

Blunders and slips

Some instances of emotional communication are unintentional. In the case of blunders, hidden emotions "slip out" at inappropriate times or the communicator misreads the emotional mood of the audience. The opening quotation from former President Bush is an example. His expression of enthusiastic support for FEMA director Brown was emotionally jarring to an American public feeling disgusted by the government's performance. The energy company Enron was destroyed by the efforts of certain executives to manipulate electricity supplies and prices. A result was that some poor and elderly consumers were forced to go without power. The company was condemned roundly when email records showed that young executives were boastful and gleeful about the success of these pernicious practices. Of course, unintended emotional messages can create positive perceptions too. The governor who reveals her "human side" by shedding a tear with disaster victims is likely to be credited for her authenticity. A salesperson who "bubbles over" with enthusiasm is assumed to be smitten with the quality of the product he sells.

Narratives

Stories are a ubiquitous form of organizational communication. The narratives told by members build and express their own identities and those of the institutions to which they are connected (Tracy, 2002). When emotional events are unexpected, heated, confusing, or rapidly evolving, stories are constructed as members make sense of things. Narratives allow these events to be mapped into a familiar form that includes heroes and villains, scripts, settings, plots, and audiences. They often include unexpected events, building suspense, and moral lessons. Many work narratives describe emotionally toxic villains, such as Ryan, the piranha-feeding manager introduced in chapter 1 (Frost, 2003). These characters are often described as unfeeling, merciless, jealous, or explosive. Emotional heroes are portrayed as compassionate (Frost, Dutton, Worline, and Wilson, 2000). Sometimes they are fearless.

When she attended law school in the New England region, Rachel worked as a researcher in a law office specializing in international litigation. She told this story:

> After I had been there about six months, I had submitted some work to a senior partner. When he came to review the work with me, he was very upset and started yelling: "What did I think I was doing? Was I trying to get him sued?" Then in the process of yelling, he threw the entire file at me! The papers separated and went flying all over the office. He never really gave me a chance to speak and all I could manage in response to his accusations was "no." I was in shock. There were other people in the office at the time. Of course, none of them said anything during or after the incident. After a while, I looked up the evidence that backed up my work. Then I calmly walked into his office and showed it to him. At that point he told me he felt like a real jerk. My response was, "well, you should."

Rachel's story makes sense of an emotional situation that developed rapidly and unexpectedly. The callous and out-of-control senior partner is clearly the villain. Rachel plays both victim and hero, as become obvious toward the end of the story as she calmly rebuts the partner and receives his expression of remorse. Her closing remark, "Well, you should," allows her to express the contempt she feels for him. Fellow employees are cast in unattractive roles. It seems important to Rachel's story that they made no empathetic remarks. They were apparently fearful or simply impassive.

The telling and retelling of narratives allows members to convey a sense of the emotional communication practices that define an organization's culture or an employee's career. We don't know the "truth" of Rachel's depiction of events. Did she really make that last remark or did she wish it were so? But the story seems to convey certain emotional qualities that she perceived in herself and co-workers. The narrative reminds her to better regulate her emotional behavior, now that she is a lawyer. It is part of a larger narrative about the kind of career she wants and the kind of people she is willing to work with. When her co-workers are emotionally stressed, the story helps her to see that things could be worse. By telling the story to others, she offers emotional lessons ("You are swimming with the sharks if you join that firm") and marks the occupational boundaries of acceptable behavior ("All lawyers get stressed, but that was ridiculous!").

Rituals

Organizations and their members produce and process emotion through ritualistic communication practices (see Martin, 1992). Rituals are formal cultural practices in which most communication behavior is prescribed and roles are predictable. Rituals often have clear beginnings and endings. Typically, members draw significance not so much from the messages that may be exchanged, but from the sense of collective action and the connection to a tradition or larger cause. Co-workers may come to feel a kind of transcendence from their daily concerns and concrete circumstances, and in this way rituals can have spiritual significance. Rituals emphasize collective identity rather than individual identity (Running, Woodward, and Girard, 2008). They prioritize emotional connection over cognitive processing. In organizations, rituals are organized for the purposes of venting emotion that is difficult to process under more ordinary circumstances. They may be used to create and integrate identity across cultural subgroups or to affirm the unique identity of a particular subgroup.

Rituals take a variety of forms. Workers may be invited by management to regularly scheduled gripe sessions to "unload" their feelings. Weekly department meetings may be important not just for coordinating activities, but also as ritualistic opportunities to share humor at the expense of management, express pent-up bitterness, or reinforce feelings of camaraderie and affection. Organizations sometimes plan ritualistic experiences for the work-force to create collectively felt emotions (Waldron, 2009). Sales rallies, organization-wide social gatherings, and annual messages from the CEO may be carefully engineered to achieve maximum emotional impact. Award ceremonies foster feelings of pride, admiration, and (perhaps) envy. Labor organizers and social action organizations may periodically stage rallies and marches to build solidarity, shore up resolve, and (sometimes) foment resent-ment. And, at schools, graduation ceremonies are offered each semester to create warm emotional experiences for students, their families, and school employees.

Conclusion

In this chapter I have discussed the levels and forms of emotional communication as it is practiced in work settings. In this context, emotional communication is complicated because it occurs across so many levels, from the perceptual processes of individual workers to the collective efforts of multinational organizations. It also flows across traditional boundaries, as rules and practices that shape emotions in the larger society influence the expectations and practices of the workplace. As we have seen, emotion "resides in" not just the bodies of individual workers, but also as a commu-nicative force within language and labels, interaction sequences, networks, stories, and rituals. The communication of feeling is a high-stakes activity. The misreading of emotional cues, the jarring emotional message, or the failure to appreciate the emotional needs of key audiences can all be costly mistakes. At the same time, the communication of emotion is an activity that defines the workplace in human terms as opposed to simply economic ones. It is largely through communication that we come to experience work as a source of satisfaction, pride, joy, and emotional connec-tion to others.

References

Andersen, P. A, and Guerrero, L., K. (eds) (1998). *The Handbook of Emotion and Communication*. San Diego, CA: Academic Press.

Ashford, B. and Humphrey, R. (1995). Emotion in the workplace: a reappraisal. *Human Relations*, 48: 97–125.

Bellantoni, C. (2008). Did Hilary win N.H. crying game? *The Washington Times* (January 10), p. A01.

Burgoon, J. K., and Le Poire, B. A. (1999). Nonverbal cues and interpersonal judgments: participant and observer perceptions of intimacy, dominance, composure, and formality. *Communication Monographs*, 66: 105–24.

Coupland, C., Brown, A. D., Daniels, K., and Humphreys, M. (2008). Saying it with feeling: analysing speakable emotions. *Human Relations*, 61: 327–53.

Dougherty, D., and Krone, K. J. (2002). Emotional intelligence as organizational communication: an examination of the construct. In W. B. Gudykunst (ed.), *Communication Yearbook 26*. Newbury Park, CA: Sage, pp. 202–29.

Fairhurst, G. T., and Putnam, L. (2006). Organizations as discursive constructions. *Communication Theory*, 14: 5–26.

Fineman, S. (ed.) (2000). *Emotion in Organizations* (2nd edn). London: Sage.

Frost, P. J. (2003). *Toxic Emotions at Work*. Cambridge: Harvard Business School Press.

Frost, P. J., Dutton, J. E., Worline, M. C., and Wilson, A. (2000). Narratives of compassion in organizations. In S. Fineman (ed.), *Emotion in Organizations* (2nd edn). London, Sage, pp. 25–45.

Hochschild, A. R. (1979). Emotion work, feeling rules, and social structure. *American Journal of Sociology*, 85: 551–75.

Hochschild, A. R. (1983). *The Managed Heart*. Berkeley, CA: University of California Press.

Kassing, J. (2007). Going around the boss: exploring the consequences of circumvention. *Management Communication Quarterly*, 21: 55–75.

Keltner, D. (2009). *Born To Be Good: The Science of a Meaningful Life*. New York: W. W. Norton & Company.

Keyton, J., and Smith, F. L. (2009). Distrust in leaders: dimensions, patterns, and emotional intensity. *Journal of Leadership and Organizational Studies*, 16: 6–18.

Krone, K. J. and Morgan, J. M. (2000). Emotion metaphors in management: the Chinese experience. In S. Fineman (ed.), *Emotion in Organizations* (2nd edn,). London, Sage, pp. 83–100.

Lammers, J. C., and Garcia, M. A. (2009). Exploring the concept of "profession" for organizational communication research: institutional influences in a veterinary organization. *Management Communication Quarterly*, 22: 357–84.

Martin, J. (1992). *Cultures in Organizations: Three Perspectives*. Oxford: Oxford University Press.

Maslach, C. (1982). *Burnout: The Cost of Caring*. Englewood cliffs, NJ: Prentice Hall.

Miller, K. I. and Koesten, J. (2008). Financial feeling: an investigation of emotion and communication in the workplace. *Journal of Applied Communication Research*, 36: 8–32.

Morsbach, H., and Tyler, W. J. (1986). A Japanese emotion: Amae. In R. Harre (ed.), *The Social Construction of Emotions*. Oxford: Blackwell, pp. 289–307.

Nadesan, M. H. (1997). Constructing paper dolls: the discourse of personality testing in organizational practice. *Communication Theory*, 7: 189–218.

Planalp, S. (1999). *Communicating Emotion: Social, Moral, and Political Processes*. Cambridge: Cambridge University Press.

Running, A., Woodward, L., and Girard, D. (2008). Ritual: the final expression of care. *International Journal of Nursing Practice*, 14: 303–7.

Scott, C. and Myers, K.K. (2005). The socialization of emotion: learning emotion management at the fire station. *Journal of Applied Communication Research*, 33: 67–92.

Tracy, K. (2002). *Everyday Talk: Building and Reflecting Identities*. New York: Guilford Press.

Tracy, K. (2009). How questioning constructs judge identities in appeals court: a state court hearing of a same-sex marriage appeal. *Discourse Studies*, 11: 191–221.

Tracy, S. J., and Tracy, K. (1998). Emotion labor at 911: a case study and theoretical critique. *Journal of Applied Communication Research*, 26: 390–411.

Waldron, V. (1994). Once more, *with feeling*. Reconsidering the role of emotion in work. In S. A. Deetz (ed.), *Communication Yearbook 17*. Thousand Oaks, CA: Sage Publications, pp. 388–416.

Waldron V. (2009). Emotional tyranny at work: suppressing the moral emotions. In P. Lutgen-Sandvik and B. Davenport-Sypher (eds), *Destructive Organizational Communication: Processes, Consequences, and Constructive Ways of Organizing*. New York: Routledge, pp. 9–26.

Waldron, V. and Kassing, J. K. (2011). *Managing Risk in Communication Encounters*. Thousand Oaks, CA: Sage.

Waldron, V., and Kelley, D. (2008). *Communicating Forgiveness*. Thousand Oaks, CA: Sage.

Waldron, V., and Krone, K. J. (1991). The experience and expression of emotion in the workplace: a study of a corrections organization. *Management Communication Quarterly*, 4: 287–309.

Weiner, B. (2006). *Social Motivation, Justice, and the Moral Emotions: An Attributional Approach*. Mahwah, NJ: Lawrence Erlbaum Associates.

White House (2005). President arrives in Alabama, briefed on Hurricane Katrina (September 2). Retrieved from: <http://georgewbush- whitehouse.archives.gov/news/releases/2005/09/20050902-2.html>.

Wu, T., and Hu, C. (2009). Abusive supervision and employee emotional exhaustion: dispositional antecedents and boundaries. *Group & Organization Management*, 34: 143–69.

Young, L. W. (1994). *Crosstalk and Culture in Sino-American Communication*. Cambridge: Cambridge University Press.

3

Emotional Occupations

(With Joshua Danaher)

Army Nurse: When surgery started (it was usually brain surgery) they had no idea what they would find and the [surgical] techniques weren't perfected at that time . . . It was a very slow process; once we got into a skull we stayed until the work was done to the best of our ability. We worked really long days and scary days . . . These young fellows on these litters; they were like Halloween masks; they just didn't even look human. It was [pause] really challenging.

Interviewer: How does one deal with that every day?

Army Nurse: I remember one day the hall was just so filled with litters with fellows on them with decimated faces and skulls and other body parts. . . . you had to kind of shimmy around to get down the hallway. One of the corpsmen just lost it. He just started screaming and crying and slid to the floor, actually. I remember just yelling, yelling, yelling at him that he had to get himself together and go ahead and function. What I remember him saying back to me (between gasps) was that a specific litter contained a person who he knew and had gone through basic training with, and was in fact his buddy. It was a real moment of truth when he verbalized what he did. I had to come to grips with the fact that what we were dealing with was absolutely impossible.

Interviewer: So you had to not only deal with your own feelings but with those of the corpsmen.

Army Nurse: Right, and also [with] what patients were conscious. They were really scared and you had to deal with them and try to pass some kind of confidence on to them. In a way it was so very dishonest, but it was the thing to do to give them the best chance of recovery.

64

Emotional Jobs

This excerpt is drawn from an interview with a former army nurse, recorded as part of the Veteran's History Project for the Library of Congress (Prescott, 2002). Rhona Marie Knox Prescott, an army captain who served in the Vietnam War during the 1960s, describes vividly the harrowing scenes and heroic actions that defined daily life in army field hospitals. Situated at the precarious boundaries of jungle battle zones, surgeons and nurses labored to save the lives of gravely injured soldiers. It is hard to imagine a more emotionally taxing occupation. As a supervising nurse, Prescott tended to the feelings of shattered patients and emotionally battered co-workers. Her "dishonest" displays of confidence, a practice we earlier described as surface acting, may have increased the survival rate of her patients, even as her own emotional resources were exhausted by constant exposure to trauma.

Few occupations require the heroic and heartbreaking emotional labor performed by Rhona Prescott and her colleagues in the Army Nurses corps. Yet many jobs do require emotional virtuosity of various kinds. Researchers have studied a startling variety of emotional laborers, including funeral home directors (Smith, orsey, and Mosley, 2009), detectives (Jackall, 2000), convenience store clerks (Sutton and Rafaeli, 1988), 911 operators (Tracy and Tracy, 1998), probation officers (Waldron and Krone, 1991), flight attendants (Hochschild, 1983), sex workers (Sanders, 2005), and many more. Although these jobs all require multiple skills, emotional prowess is often an important selection criterion. And, once on the job, employee success is in part an emotional matter. Promotion or demotion? Retention or termination? Leader or follower? A worker's capacity to communicate emotion influences these decisions. In some cases, the emotional requirements are only implied. "She just doesn't take direction well," reads the personnel evaluation of an employee who reacted too angrily to negative performance feedback. Other times, the evaluation criteria are explicitly emotional, as in the case of items used on some evaluations of college teachers ("The instructor shows enthusiasm for the subject matter").

So, which occupations require the most challenging kinds of emotional labor? Actually, we find emotional jobs to be so numerous that it might be easier to list those that have *limited* demands on employees' emotional resources. In this chapter, we can feature only selected occupations, those that provide particularly rich examples of the ways that communication and emotion intersect as employees perform their work. We chose some based on familiarity. Most of us have encountered teachers, salespersons, religious leaders, or 911 operators in the course of our lives. But the complicated emotional requirements of these work roles are rarely appreciated. We paid less attention to those occupations that have already received ample attention in the literature. Therefore, we don't spend much time on Disney workers or telemarketers, or detectives. In contrast, we do explore professions that most of us encounter rarely, or only indirectly, through electronic and mass media. We chose them because they are unusually influential in society or because they clearly illustrate a unique kind of emotional performance. Some are unusual or even a bit exotic: talk-show hosts, self-help gurus, comedians, and drill sergeants.

In analyzing occupations, we look past some of the traditional criteria, such as the amount of education required or the time spent on certain kinds of physical or cognitive tasks. Instead, we consider the kinds of emotional performance required of job occupants. Table 3.1 lists these occupational categories, selected jobs in each grouping, and typical functions of emotional communication as it is practiced by these kinds of workers. For example, in the boundary workers category, we include receptionists, sales clerks, and servers. As noted in the table, these workers often regulate emotion as it flows from customers and the public into the organization (and vice versa). They also frequently perform "surface acting" (chapter 1; see also Hochschild, 1983), the fabrication of emotion in response to job requirements. In another example, we list certain kinds of salespeople under the category "emotional believers," as they come to develop a genuine emotional affinity for a product or service. This we called "deep acting" in chapter 1.

Toward the end of the chapter we note that, when it comes to emotional communication tasks, some employees are the equiva-

Table 3.1 Emotional occupations: categories, illustrative jobs, and communication functions

Category	Illustrative jobs	Selected emotional functions
Boundary spanners	Receptionist, clerk, server	Regulate flow, read cues, surface acting, smooth out transactions
Emotional believers	Salesperson, hospice worker, flight attendant	Deep acting, self-talk, internalization
Prescribers	Teacher, mediator, public relations staff, human resources officer	Instruct, direct, advise, correct
Elicitors	Film-maker, stand-up comic, police officer	Surprise, shock, scare, amuse
Resilience builders	Drill sergeant, medical intern, trainer	Anticipate, protect, toughen
Orchestrators	Coach, manager, leader, funeral director	encourage, "charge up," sustain, facilitate mourning
Coolers and soothers	911 operator, crisis manager, con artist	calm, dissipate, soothe
Guides and seekers	Clergy, guru, cult leader	Devise rituals, deepen feeling, inspire, transcend the mundane
Moral emoters	Activist, cable television host, political campaign designer	evoke outrage, shame opponents
"Utility players"	not job-specific	Toxin handling, mood shifting; articulating

lent of "utility" players in baseball, the relatively few individuals who are flexible enough in their skills to play multiple positions on the team. They may be trained in a given occupation, but they are capable of performing any number of the communication tasks that keep an organization on a sound emotional footing. Their emotional labor is not job-specific. As examples, we consider the tasks of toxin handling, mood shifting, and emotional articulation. Finally, we offer observations on occupational socialization, the lifelong process of learning the emotional expectations that define what it means to be a professional. Certainly, some of our emotional communication is learned on the job at the behest of our current employers. But emotional socialization begins early in life, as future employees participate in family life and absorb the emotional practices of the culture to which they belong.

Surface Acting and Boundary Work: Meet the "Director of First Impressions"

Many emotion workers find themselves positioned at the boundaries of their organizations. These front-line employees are your first point of contact when you enter a retail store, doctor's office, or restaurant. Their occupational titles include receptionists, greeters, hosts, and front-desk clerks. Trusted by their organizations to create a pleasant first impression, these workers spend their days enacting ritual, engaging in repeated, brief, and highly predictable interactions. They welcome clients who are expected and discourage those who lack an appointment. They provide directions to the lost and provide information to the confused. But, most importantly, by enacting a pleasant, calm demeanor, these emotion workers maintain a kind of emotional firewall between the organization and its public. Boundary workers prevent visitors from stumbling unannounced upon the emotional antics of employees – their fiery conflicts or giddy expressions of triumph. At the same time, they serve as a buffer to the emotions that blow through the front door in the form of impatient clients, dissatisfied customers, or fearful patients.

Cici was the receptionist at a suburban junior high school. At least she was until her school district adopted a comprehensive customer service improvement program offered by a consulting company. Now she is the "Director of First Impressions." Despite the title change, Cici reports that her job duties are basically the same, "to manage the traffic at the front office, keep the parents happy, and protect the administrators from too many distractions." When observed more closely, her work day appears to involve a variety of forms of emotional labor. First, she must sustain an impression of cheerful pleasantness at all times, even at the end of a long day, even when parents are rude, even when the airspace in front of her desk is besieged with questions hurled in her direction by unruly children and harried teachers.

Second, Cici must diagnose the emotional states of visitors as she determines how to direct them. An angry parent enters the office, demanding to see a teacher. Should the parent first be directed to the assistant principle for a "cooling off" talk? Should Cici surreptitiously notify the campus safety officer? Or would a bit of stalling and light-hearted conversation calm the parent and yield an improved understanding of the situation? As the Director of First Impressions, Cici's third task is to communicate the emotions she observes around her. The school principal may need to know that a visiting administrator "appears upset," the teacher waiting for an appointment is anxious, the student who is awaiting discipline for a playground infraction is displaying a remorseful countenance.

Cici's work, and that of other emotional boundary spanners, is often characterized by a rapid pace and multitasking. They must invest enough communicative effort in each visitor to establish a warm and pleasant first impression, but they rarely have time for extended conversation. Indeed, their communication often occurs against the backdrop of phones waiting to be answered, customers waiting their turn, and fellow employees waiting for answers to their queries. All of this creates an atmosphere of urgency and impatience. The results of an interesting study reveal the dilemma faced by emotional boundary spanners (Sutton and Rafeli, 1988). The researchers observed systematically the emotional displays by convenience-store clerks and correlated them with sales data. It turns out that positive emotional behavior (such as small talk and smiling) goes only so far in the rapid-fire transactions performed by these workers. Although surly or obnoxious clerks would not be appreciated by convenience-store customers, these visitors put a premium on transaction speed. They want to make their purchases and be on their way. So it was clerks who processed transactions most quickly, not those who engaged in pleasant small talk, who were most successful in raising sales.

However, boundary workers who make the most of their brief encounters are often appreciated by fellow employees who find their own jobs have been made easier. This is particularly true when (unlike the convenience-store context) the organization must sustain a long-term relationship with members of the public and when visitors are passed on to other employees. For example, at even the busiest times, a skilled restaurant hostess/host will put impatient customers in a positive frame of mind as they are steered to their seats. Accordingly, their server will find them easier to please and may receive larger tips. Back in the school context, Cici is "worth her weight in gold" according to her boss, who finds that even the most disgruntled parents are more constructive after spending a few minutes with the Director of First Impressions. These observations reinforce our point: emotional boundary managers strike a delicate balance between emotional attentiveness and efficiency.

Emotional Believers: Deep Acting and the Education of Book Salespersons

Based on her early observations of emotional laborers in various fields, Arlie Hochschild (1983) distinguished between surface and deep acting. In the former, workers learn to fake their emotions – to display good cheer even when they feel depressed or sullen. But deep acting involves a more significant level of emotional transformation. Employees learn to actually feel the emotion required by their occupations. Once sufficiently socialized to their professional roles, workers come to experience the expected emotions effortlessly and apparently genuinely. Emotional training can be a critical part of the organizational socialization process (for a detailed review, see Kramer, 2010). Workers internalize emotions along with values, rules, language practices, and other dimensions of organizational culture. Of course, organizations often *select* new employees who appear predisposed to experience the expected emotions. Chosen for their enthusiasm for the company's services, calm demeanor, or the pride they take in their work, these newcomers may respond more readily to emotional training. It is important to note that workers are not merely passive recipients of socialization who simply step into existing work roles. Rather, some employees actively shape their new roles, adjusting these based on their own experiences, strengths, and personal dispositions. The enthusiastic new employee who is labeled a "breath of fresh air" by senior colleagues would be just one example. All of this is to say that deep acting emerges from a process of learning as employees and organizations internalize the emotions required by the work. In some ways much akin to the boot-camp experiences of soldiers, medical training tries to prepare newcomers for the kinds of emotionally intense experiences that they could never have encountered, perhaps never even imagined, in a more ordinary working life.

Deep acting is evident in numerous professions. For example, hospice workers must learn to remain compassionate even when they know all of their patients will die. Faced constantly with the prospect of death, they must put aside feelings of fear or pity even as they remain emotionally engaged with patients and their families. Interestingly, according to the authors of a recent study, hospice nurses who are discouraged from expressing their own grief may be more prone to emotional burnout and "compassion fatigue" (Running, Woodward, and Girard, 2008). However, by participating in "grief rituals," these employees retain the capacity to express grief in healthy ways. The researchers observed a weekly ritual in which workers honored the passing of their patients, shared memories, and offered support. The meeting was initiated and ended with the sounding of a gong, and the sacred and serious nature of the occasion was acknowledged with music or poetry. In this way, the hospice staff could genuinely experience feelings of loss and sustain real (rather than "faked") feelings of compassion.

A different but common kind of deep acting is that associated with sales occupations (for an interesting ethnography, see Prus,

1989). The example below describes the experiences of "Dan," a young college student who was training for the emotionally difficult work of door-to-door sales (Waldron and Kassing, 2011: 48–9). Dan and other "cold sellers" must learn to be unfailingly enthusiastic in the face of constant rejection. Through a ritualistic kind of training, offered to thousands of college students every summer, they develop a deeply felt confidence in their product and their own capacity to make the sale. As with other forms of deep acting, Dan's newly acquired emotional orientation affected his relationships outside of work. Those who knew him well detected a fundamental change in his identity.

Dan was fairly typical of students at his rural state university. While browsing for summer jobs at the Career Center, Dan's eye settled on an eye-popping advertisement for a lucrative summer job selling Bibles and encyclopedias. Dan applied for and got the job. After classes ended in May, Dan found himself driving to a remote location in the Deep South, where he and thousands of other students would attend sales boot camp – intensive training in the emotional art of door-to-door book selling. For days, Dan and his colleagues were subjected to highly emotional speeches by legendary salespeople, all of whom exhorted the students to embrace a positive attitude. Students were taught that sales success turned on the power of an unending smile and the charm of a cheerful demeanor. After a week of nearly around-the-clock exposure to this barrage of positivity, Dan's easygoing personality and natural caution, his nagging doubts about his promise as a salesperson, were transformed into a sunny sense of self-confidence and an unswerving commitment to eliminate doubt and negativity from not just his work, but his relationships with other people.

Dan spent a trying summer slogging with two other young men across the humid Midwest, making barely enough money to cover their expenses. Despite facing rejection at nearly every front door, Dan's positive outlook never failed. He simply hadn't learned to be positive enough – that was the explanation for the poor sales results.

Dan's family and his girlfriend noticed a change in him that fall. He was resolutely positive at even the most trying times. He offered a hearty handshake to anyone he encountered. Dan refused to socialize with "negative people" and preferred not to share feelings like frustration and anger. Amazed at his new confidence and outgoing personality, family members couldn't help wondering if it all was "real." Had they gained a salesman at the cost of the son and sibling they knew so well? Years later, Dan is a highly successful sales agent. Dan's many acquaintances enjoy his sunny demeanor and unfailingly positive outlook. He never loses his cool or brings them down.

Emotion Prescribers: The Curious Case of "Dr Phil"

A primary communication function of some occupations is instructing others in the emotion that they "should be" feeling. Elementary school teachers do this as they help young students learn when to feel proud of their work, ashamed of their behavior, or happy for the accomplishments of others. However, we find that the "prescription" metaphor, drawn from medicine, is more broadly applicable, as it extends beyond teachers to the broader set of professions in which the shaping of others' emotion is a central task. The metaphor implies that one person (the patient) is experiencing symptoms that will be alleviated if she adopts healthier emotional habits, as prescribed by an expert, such as a doctor, motivational speaker, mediator, advisor, or even the cheerleader at a sporting event. The prescriber may perceive that the patient is overindulging in unhealthy emotions or failing to experience those deemed to be necessary or healthy. Emotion prescribers are judges of normal and abnormal emotion. They are often keen observers of the emotional status quo and they are quick to recognize "deviations" and offer corrective advice. These professionals know that emotions can motivate constructive or destructive behavior. For example, professional mediators may prescribe a "cooling off" period when negotiations become too heated. Politicians are notorious emotion prescribers, particularly when they demand that their opponents display more patriotic feelings or urge their followers to feel outraged about the latest scandal involving their opponents.

Many readers will be familiar with Dr Phil, a frequent guest on daytime talk shows, famous for dispensing advice and admonitions to struggling lovers and confused parents. Dr Phil is unique in the sense that his emotional labor occurs before an audience – in the studio and watching on television. Indeed, his ability to manipulate their emotions, to whip up collective feelings of indignation or compassion, accounts for his strong ratings. As noted in critical commentaries of his performances, Dr Phil's brand of on-air talk therapy features a domineering, masculine persona, one which exudes the message: "I will take charge of this out-of-control situation" (for an intriguing analysis, see Henson and Parameswaran, 2008). For our purposes, Dr Phil can be characterized as the prototypical emotion prescriber. That is, a large part of his work is convincing clients to feel guilt, compassion, indignation, fear, and other emotions that Dr Phil believes would be "good for them" and their relationships. In a recent TV consultation (CBS News, 2007), the popular therapist illustrated each of the four tasks typically performed by emotional prescribers. In this case, a mother shared her exasperation with her daughter's dangerous habit of texting while driving. Mom wanted the TV therapist to talk some sense into her haughty and recalcitrant teenager.

As an emotional prescriber, Dr Phil's first task was to reinforce his credibility, to establish a certain gravitas. He did so by addressing the girl with a solemn, stern voice and a patriarchic countenance – as if to signal that she (and the studio audience) should be in awe of his credentials, which were in obvious contrast to those of her ineffectual mother. An emotional prescriber's second task is to offer the diagnosis. Dr Phil established that the daughter's irresponsible driving behavior was the problem. He did so by reciting, with a growing sense of disgust, a long list of her traffic citations. He reprimanded the girl, "You may think that it's okay to do that, but you don't have the right to do that!" In emotional terms, Dr Phil humiliated his young guest and shamed her in front of the now indignant studio audience. The third task is to establish consequences for non-compliance. He warned the young driver. If she failed to change her texting behavior, fearful consequences would follow. He instilled fear by reminding her that real people (his relatives, her relatives) could be killed by drivers just like her. Finally, emotional prescribers must assure continued compliance with the prescribed course of action. They can do so by boosting confidence ("You can do it!"), cultivating feelings of responsibility and guilt ("We are counting on you to shape up"), or stoking feelings of fear ("If I catch you doing this again, there will be hell to pay"). Dr Phil chose the second of these options.

In summary, Dr Phil prescribed a sequence of emotional experiences for the texting teenaged driver – awe, humiliation, fear, and continuing guilt. In doing so, he was aided by a supporting cast – his studio audience. In this sense, his emotional labor is quite different from the medical doctor who dashes off a quick prescription for an antibiotic. It is more akin to a multistep medical intervention, one that cultivates "healthier" emotions and urges the patient to cease unhealthy behavior. Of course, other professionals issue emotional prescriptions as part of their work. The human resources officer may be called in when employees need directions on the kinds of emotion that counts as "professional" and "unprofessional." Theater and movie directors dictate emotions that actors should be feeling in a given scene. Public relations specialists may prescribe a dose of humility or remorse to clients who are trying to repair a damaged image before an observant public.

Emotion Elicitors: Stand-up Comics, Film-makers, and Police Officers

One way that communication and emotion are linked is through acts of elicitation. Unlike prescribers, who know which emotions we should be feeling and command us to feel them, elicitors create the conditions that may (or may not) lead the listener to feel voluntarily certain kinds of emotion. Through the skillful use of language and non-verbal behavior, they help us see the world from a particular perspective. "Seeing that way" leads us to feel certain emotions, such as compassion, hilarity, or fear. Elicitors are sophisticated observers of human experience and they catalog the connections between circumstances and emotions. For example, the makers of horror films know that a delicious kind of shrieking fear can be elicited from audience members when, safely ensconced in their seats, they are transported to a setting rife with ghoulish villains, mounting anticipation, unpredictable and bloody plot twists, and crashing musical scores. For the most part, viewers are willing participants. But their emotions must be elicited by the film-maker's craft. Otherwise the film (and the emotion) falls flat. Indeed, some films "work too hard" to gain an emotional response and the audience leaves the theater feeling manipulated, drained, or cheated.

Stand-up comedians perform a similar kind of emotional elicitation, although they do so in real time, with a sometimes unpredictable audience. Comedian Bernadette Pauley works nightclubs and the college comedy circuit. In a recent interview (Pauley, 2010) posted on the Comedy Central website, she explored her occupation with host Christian Thom. According to this successful stand-up artist, the key is to create an emotional chemistry with the audience. She does it in a three-step process. The first task is to empathize with the audience, to show an understanding of their daily routines, relational expectations, pleasures, and frustrations. Second, the comedian disrupts the audience's sense of reality by introducing such elements as exaggeration, absurdity, sarcasm, and irony. This violation of expectations and routine makes it possible for the listener to put aside everyday worries and negative emotions. The resulting emotional space is filled by feelings of surprise, camaraderie, and glee.

For stand-up comedians, the second task is practice. Eliciting these emotions requires skilled use of physical gestures, tone of voice, audience vocabulary, and timing. The third task is adapting in real time to audience feedback such as knowing laughter or awkward silence. For example, Pauley adjusts her use of "marriage material" with college audiences. "I don't even start talking about being married until a half an hour has passed. It gives them a chance to get to know me and who I am . . . I guess it's a little like boxing; you do a little 'jab, jab' and you move them over into your territory." Her boxing analogy may be apt because Pauley often has the audience shedding tears of laughter by the end of her knockout performances.

76

In a very different occupational realm, police work often involves the elicitation of emotion (Jackall, 2000). Formally and informally, officers learn to use verbal and non-verbal behavior for such purposes as intimidating crime suspects or calming hysterical witnesses (e.g., Kidwell, 2006). Emotion is sometimes elicited through collaborative efforts, as when interrogators use the "good cop–bad cop" technique. The cooperative efforts of officers, attorneys, and judge create an aura of "grim formality" in courtrooms, which may leave unseasoned defendants and their families feeling awed or terrified (Waldron, 2000). In each of these cases, the emotional experience is not so much prescribed by an expert or by convention (see "emotional prescribers" above) as it is brought forth by an intentional manipulation of messages and circumstances.

Emotional Meaning Makers: Clergy, Gurus, and a "Spiritual Warrior"

As we have discussed, the routines of work can dull our emotions and curtail opportunities to communicate the diversity of human feeling. Many people deepen and diversify their emotional experience by participating in religious practices, attending artistic performances, or subjecting themselves to demanding physical regimens (such as yoga or marathon running). These activities serve multiple purposes, but most allow participants to transcend the mundane and the secular, while connecting to the meaningful and spiritual. Roughly 42 percent of Americans report attending religious services on a weekly basis (Gallup, 2010). Emotion is a key feature of religious services. Depending on the denomination, worshipers may report such varied experiences as "feeling close to God," guilt, hope, humility before God's creation, love and compassion, spiritual renewal, or the courage to confront evil.

Religious professionals guide attendees through these emotional journeys. The Bureau of Labor Statistics (2008) reported that more than 42,000 clergy work in the United States (not including those who are self-employed). These religious leaders often create sacred emotional experiences by organizing rituals and facilitating transcendent encounters through such activities as chanting, singing, ritual cleansing, speaking in tongues, and many others. They help followers make sense of the sometimes profound emotions that accompany religious exploration.

For so many persons, the search for sacred emotional experiences is meaningful and rewarding. But some do have acutely negative reactions when they come under the influence of spiritual guides. Around the time this chapter was written (spring, 2011), newspaper headlines reported shocking details about the activities of James Arthur Ray, a self-styled spiritual guru practicing in Sedona, Arizona. Ray's controversial "Spiritual Warrior" programs were psychologically and physically intensive spiritual boot camps attended by an apparently well-educated, enthusiastic, and mostly well-off group of spiritual seekers. Yet, by the end of the most recent session, two people were dead and 19 injured after subjecting themselves to an excruciating "sweat lodge" ceremony of Ray's design. The tragedy is a cautionary tale, as it highlights how people with a hunger for seemingly transcendent emotional experiences must be careful in choosing leaders to guide them.

Although the details are not fully known, Ray's Spiritual Warrior program seems to have involved five communication tasks that are commonly facilitated by spiritual guides. First, the guide helps identify feelings of isolation or meaninglessness, as James Arthur Ray apparently did in seminars designed to recruit emotionally unfulfilled people to his Angel Valley retreat center. Second, potential adherents are offered an enticing vision of a more fulfilling and authentic spiritual life. Ray cloaked his inspirational message in the language of Native American religious traditions. Advertising for his Sedona center promised "a place to relax and heal . . . where powerful earth energies are present and active" (quoted in Katz, 2009). In this way, potential clients glimpsed a starkly different and richer emotional climate. A process of initiation is the third step, where recruits are asked to offer sacrifices and/or pledges as a signal that they are committed to the cause. Emotionally, this step prepares recruits to join the community of fellow seekers. It may involve a casting off of habits, public confessions, or a pledge of financial resources. James urged his adherents to put aside their limiting assumptions and skepticism while investing thousands of dollars to attend his programs. A fourth step is emotional purification, whereby participants are made emotionally ready for their role in the spiritual community. Spiritual Warriors spent a night alone in the forest, as a way of overcoming their fear and demonstrating that they had the courage to be spiritual warriors. Importantly, Ray provided steady emotional support for his well-heeled clients as they negotiated this trying transition. As one visitor wrote, "I felt welcome and special by the way all your staff opened your hearts to us. Everyone went out of their way to make us feel comfortable and loved. Thank you for easing me along the next step of my journey."

The culminating task involves an intense ritual of emotional bonding with the leader and other seekers. Ray's final step in building the courage of his spiritual warriors involved appropriation of the sweat-lodge ceremony from Native American tradition. His followers were subjected to hours-long immersion in a stultifying "lodge" constructed from a ragged assortment of building materials and covered with tarps. According to law enforcement officials, Ray created a climate of intimidation which discouraged even obviously ill adherents from leaving and able-bodied attendees from helping their ill comrades. Ray denies the charges. He awaits trial in Arizona.

Emotional Resilience Builders: Trainers, Drill Sergeants, and Medical Students

As Arlie Hochschild (1983) noted long ago, emotional fabrication, or "surface acting," is a taxing form of labor. If they are to sustain a smiling demeanor in the face of surly clients, impatient citizens, and emotionally abusive customers, service workers must prepare themselves. Disney's much-emulated training programs do this by convincing workers they are crucial performers in the "greatest show on earth" (Waldron, 1994). Emotional abuse is a small price to pay for the opportunity to be in show business, so cast members are expected to appreciate the opportunity to engage in sustained emotional fakery – it is all part of being an actor. The "role" may eventually appear less glamorous, as the actors spend long days pushing brooms and cleaning up the vomit left in the wake of overstimulated children. But there is no doubt that Disney trainers have some modicum of success in building the emotional resilience of employees.

Sex workers may prepare for their own emotionally demanding work with a similar approach – by constructing a "manufactured identity." Sanders (2005) reported the results of an ethnographic study of female sex workers in Britian's prostitution markets. She found that some workers viewed their craft as "just acting" – a way of framing their work that allowed them to accept money by manipulating the erotic expectations of male clients. As with Disney workers, this bit of identity management allowed the prostitutes to divorce their real feelings from the emotional fabrication required of their work. Doing so allowed them to persist in labor that otherwise might take a prohibitive emotional toll.

The development of emotional resilience in others is a crucial component of other familiar professions, one which extends well beyond the confines of service work. Perhaps no occupation requires more emotional resilience than that of the combat soldier. In sometimes harrowing battle conditions, soldiers are asked to display courage while controlling fear. They are taught to remain "cool under fire" and must put aside the feelings of compassion that ordinarily keep humans from killing. Faced with horrific scenes – the maiming of close comrades or the unintended deaths of innocent civilians – soldiers are required to suppress emotional reactions of shock, sympathy, or pity. The grueling emotional demands of war can take a great toll on soldiers on the battlefield and after their return to civilian life, when many grapple with post-traumatic stress disorder (PTSD) and other mental health challenges.

Preparing soldiers for the emotional extremes of war is the job of military trainers, including the drill sergeants, who (at least as portrayed in popular films) "toughen up" raw recruits by subjecting them to a steady stream of verbal abuse, unyielding regulations, and exhausting fitness regimens. In this traditional approach, military training strengthen a soldier's *emotional armor* in the hopes of preventing a "crack" in his or her composure when confronted with battle conditions.

What are the key occupational tasks of emotional arming? The first is to cultivate ways of thinking that will help soldiers manage their emotions. Disciplined soldiers are less likely to experience uncertainty and panic under chaotic wartime conditions. The second task is to cultivate emotional bonds among comrades. An emotional "esprit de corps" is constructed through standardization in dress and living conditions, unifying symbols (medals, awards), inspirational narratives of bravery and sacrifice, the cultivation of patriotism and pride, and the sense of a common enemy. Finally, the troops must be "inoculated" against some of the emotions that accompany war, by exposing them to stressful conditions and training them to channel emotions such as fear and regret into aggressive responses that will neutralize a threat. "War games" provide this most advanced form of emotional arming.

A new and different approach is designed to foster the "emotional resiliency" in soldiers, 20 percent of whom have been experiencing mental health problems after returning from recent wars in Iraq and Afghanistan (Carey, 2009). Drawing on principles of positive psychology, the program teaches soldiers to rethink faulty assumptions that lead to such emotions as anger, frustration, or despair. One such thought pattern is the tendency to assume the worst under conditions of uncertainty. For example, the soldier who receives a busy signal when calling his girlfriend back home might worry that she is talking with an old flame. This soldier would be encouraged to think about the more realistic explanation – she is simply on the phone with a family member or friend. In another example, soldiers learn that survivors of stressful situations do not always experience PTSD. Many actually develop emotional resiliency that will serve them well later in life. In these ways, military personnel are asked to reframe their cognitive perspectives, to imagine more positive interpretations, and to talk about emotions before acting on them. The hope is that positive emotions and improved mental health will follow.

This brand of emotional resilience training may be complicated by the organizational norms of military culture. Soldiers are not typically asked to talk about emotions. In fact, doing so is sometimes associated with weaknesses, psychological coddling, and shame. When interviewed by a *New York Times* reporter about the program, the general in charge of the program worried, "I am still not sure that our culture is ready to accept this" (Carey, 2009). However, it appears that the US military is altering its view of emotion. Rather than viewing it as a crack in a soldier's armor, military trainers are preparing soldiers to engage their emotions and express them in healthier ways.

The socialization of medical doctors offers an additional example of intense emotional preparation. In the US, doctors in training experience several intense years of hands-on learning after they complete mandatory classroom instruction. Working practically around-the-clock, often teetering on the brink of exhaustion, these medical residents interview patients, assist with surgeries, dispense medical instructions, and make every effort to absorb the expertise of their more experienced colleagues. Long hours of exposure to the physical and emotional trauma experienced by patients helps neophyte physicians develop a certain hardiness, perhaps even a sense of detachment, that may later serve them well when they must face alone the stresses of surgery or a relentless stream of sick patients. In short, the training builds emotional resilience along with medical prowess. The experience of medical education is so life-altering that it has inspired a number of powerful biographies (e.g., Klass, 1987). But the work can be interpersonally daunting and part of a doctor's medical education is learning to safeguard her or his own emotional health. The physician and writer Perry Klass described it this way, in her *Treatment Kind and Fair: Letters to a Young Doctor* (2007), a collection of essays addressed to her son.

I have learned to protect myself a little – to understand that the tragedy is happening to the patient, and not to me, and that my job is to focus on the job and on helping, not on my own emotions (p. 46).

Emotion Orchestrators: Athletic Coaches, Funeral Directors, and Managers

> Shock tactics or ploys such as bull castration and frog dismembering, can be self-defeating.
>
> Advice to coaches on motivational locker-room speeches (Wilson, 1996)

The reader will be relieved to read that bull castration is discouraged these days, but coaching competitive athletes remains an intense occupation, in part because the work requires constant manipulation of the emotions of coach, athletes, opponents, and fans (for more on the coach–athlete relationships, see Kassing and Barber, 2007). Even casual sports fans have witnessed the chaotic scrum of football players huddling before a game, shouting themselves into a frenzy of emotion, smacking shoulder pads and butting heads until they charge the field like some crazed swarm of killer bees. Behind that burst of emotion, sometimes smack in the middle of it, is the coach, the master motivator – what we have come to call an *emotion charger*. Joe Fusco, a football coach at Westminster College (PA), describes this motivational dimension of the work: "Preparation and *hard work* are the keys to success ... But the athlete must also *want* to do the task. Without the motivation to act, all [her or] his preparation and work would come to nothing" (Wilson, 1996; italics and parenthetical material added). As emotional laborers, coaches assess the emotional temperature of individual players and entire teams and adapt their communicative strategies to incite, sustain, or dampen emotional intensity.

What does this variety of emotional labor entail? The first task may be to envision the emotional requirements of athletic success.

What emotions must athletes experience if they are to work as a successful team by the end of the season? For Coach Fusco that means instilling pride in his players and creating excitement about their prospects for collective success (Wilson, 1996). Second, successful coaches choreograph the emotional trajectory of a season even as they make adjustments on the fly. Teams shouldn't peak too early, lose steam after a disappointing setback, or feel intimidated when faced with a daunting opponent. Instead, they should build confidence as the season progresses, develop a sense of controlled intensity, and display poise during big games. Coaches prepare schedules and design practices to help their players make these kinds of emotional progress.

As the season unfolds, the third task is the ongoing assessment of the "emotional temperature" of a player or team. Does an underperforming starter need to be benched to reignite her competitive fire? Will a lethargic team respond to a rousing locker-room speech or an exaggerated display of disappointment by a sulking coach? The fourth task involves the period immediately before a competition. How will the coach prepare the team for intimidating foes? Will it be necessary to work the team into a competitive fury or is it the calming of overwrought nerves that is called for? Can the emotional tone of the team be honed to provide a competitive edge? During the game comes the fifth occupational task – interactively managing emotions as they wax and wane over the course of the competition. A coach may adopt an exaggerated sense of calm, erupt in arm-waving frustration at the referees, remove the opponent's momentum by calling a "time out," or regulate the feelings of his own players by chastising them for excessive emotional displays. During the game, coaches manage the emotion of the audience by "whooping up" the fans or remaining indifferent to insults and taunts hurled by a hostile crowd. A sixth task follows the game, as the coach helps players manage and interpret feelings of disappointment or elation. In offering a post-game analysis, the coach cues the players to feel pride or shame in their performance or determination to do better next time. Later, as the game fades in memory, coaches help players heal emotionally and find hope in the team's future prospects. And, as the next game approaches, the coach seeks the correct emotional formula. The charging cycle begins anew.

This kind of sustained and elaborate orchestration of feelings is crucial in a number of professions. Perhaps most visible are the efforts of leaders and managers, often called "coaches" in the parlance of some organizations, particularly those organized around "teams," who find themselves called to perform tasks similar to their counterparts in athletics. Defining acceptable emotional displays, building enthusiasm, sustaining morale, managing disappointment, "lighting a fire" under unmotivated employees – these are among the many emotional functions served by leaders as they orchestrate not just a successful season, but the longer-term success of a team or organization.

Funeral directors engage in emotional orchestration of a different sort (Smith, Dorsey, and Mosley, 2009). Among many other things, these professionals create processes and rituals that help people manage their emotional responses to death. The process unfolds over time, as grieving relatives meet face-to-face with the funeral director to "make arrangements" for coffins, burial or cremation practices, obituaries, and ceremonies. Skilled funeral directors find ways to help mourners define their emotions, express them, modulate them, and share them with others in appropriate ceremonies. They orchestrate emotion by enveloping mourners and their supporters in carefully managed environments which, depending on religious and cultural tradition, might be comprised of the funeral chapel, flowers, grave offerings (items to accompany the dead in the coffin), artifacts (pictures of the deceased), costuming (staff dressed in black), music, and memory artifacts (obituaries, guest books, a visual narrative of the life led by the deceased). All of these serve as emotional cues and are designed to lead mourners though an emotional process of grieving.

Coolers and Soothers: Crisis Workers, Counselors, and Con Artists

Some forms of emotional labor call for the skill of calming, cooling, or defusing the emotions experienced by others. For example, 911 operators take calls from people who may be frightened to the point of hysteria (for an exemplary study of this profession, see Tracy and Tracy, 1998). Calming them down makes it more likely that accurate information can be obtained. For people in personal crisis, counselors may help feelings of despair or anger dissipate to some degree. A temporary emotional intervention may assist the client consider more dispassionately the options at his or her disposal and their possible consequences. Similarly, when a company experiences a crisis because its product caused harm to the public, or its executives became embroiled in scandal, experts in crisis communication are called upon. Their job is to placate or calm the public (and the press) by creating an appearance of composure, offering messages of contrition or compassion, and conveying a sense of confidence about the future. All of these jobs require a certain expertise in cooling down an emotionally hot situation.

Counselors, psychologists, and social workers play a variety of important roles. But one of them is to soothe and calm those who are emotionally distressed. This work often involves empathetic listening. The counselor's office can be a private and safe place to vent emotions that otherwise might go unexpressed. The counselor may help a client explore emotions that have been unnamed, puzzling, or unfamiliar, and in doing so can offer assurance that such feelings are normal, healthy, or manageable. By helping clients communicate emotions, these professionals may help them feel more in control of their lives.

A peculiar but interesting form of emotional cooling was documented long ago by Erving Goffman, the influential sociologist who carefully observed the daily interactions of a wide range of interesting professionals, including those who worked in "asylums for the insane" and illegal gambling operations. One of his more interesting studies involved observations of "con artists, those who lured an investor (whom they labeled the 'mark') to invest money in ethically questionable gambling ventures" (Goffman, 1952). He described the process this way in a passage that assumes the "mark" is a male:

> The potential sucker [the "mark"] is first spotted and one member of the working team . . . arranges to make social contact with him. The confidence of the mark is won, and he is given the opportunity to invest money in the gambling venture which is understood to be fixed in his favor. The venture, of course, is fixed, but not in his favor. The mark is permitted to win some money and then persuaded to invest more. There is an "accident" or a "mistake" and the mark loses the total investment. The operators then depart in a ceremony called the blowoff or sting. The mark is expected to go on his way, a little wiser and a lot poorer. (p. 451; also quoted in Waldron, 2000: 76).

Upon discovering that they have been duped, some suckers are embarrassed or ashamed by their involvement in a shady venture. They go away quietly. But others are so outraged by the deception that they threaten to "squawk" to the police, a move the con artists consider "bad for business" because it draws attention to their clandestine activities. In these cases, one of the operators, the "cooler," stays behind to calm down the mark and convince him or her to accept his or her fate. Marks are convinced that their own greed is to blame for loss of money. They are told that the police will hold the mark accountable, perhaps more so than the con artists. The cooler may emphasize the shame that would be experienced by the mark if family and friends discovered their involvement in questionable activities. These communicative efforts, what Goffman calls "cooling the mark out" are designed to dissipate feelings of disappointment and indignation while intensifying guilt, shame, and fear. Ultimately, this is an act of self-protection for the operators, as it assures that shady dealings will remain secret.

Self-protection is a requirement of other, less odious, professions where the disappointed clients may feel they have been misled, cheated, or harmed. Consider the stockbroker who steers a trusting client to a company whose value immediately plummets, the surgeon who fails to fully cure a patient, the car dealer who sells a "lemon." In each case, client expectations have been violated and they may vent their rage at the professional. At that point, the cooling-out process must begin. Perhaps the client can be convinced that the stock will recover, the patient can be assured that he or she will feel better in time, the car buyer can be assuaged by an offer of free repairs. In each case, a key occupational skill is to "cool out" emotion.

Moral Emoters: Social Activists, Politicians, and Cable Television Hosts

When employees tell stories about unjust treatment, emotions are typically an important element of the narrative (Harlos and Pinder, 2000). The emotion is sometimes identified as the cause of injustice, as when a supervisor directs a withering outburst of angry expletives at her employees. Often the emotion is a reaction to injustice; a co-worker expresses indignation at the favoritism he perceives in his workgroup. Still other times, the emotional tenor of an organization's culture may feel "wrong." For example, a young doctor may be put off by the degree of emotional detachment exhibited by her more experienced colleagues, or workers may tire of the "hysterical" reactions of management every time sales figures fall even slightly. In chapter 5, these connections between emotion and organizational morality are explored in detail. Here we consider emotion workers who make a living by eliciting moral emotions from various constituents.

Social activists arouse such emotions as indignation, fear, mortification, outrage, or guilt as part of their efforts to mobilize voters and protestors. They must be adept at using the mass media if they are to tap the moral emotions of a large audience. An example of this is found in a widely viewed television advertisement aired during the early days of the environmental movement. Featuring a traditionally clad Native American male, the ad tried to shame viewers into taking action against pollution. As he gazed at a once pristine landscape, now desecrated by trash and industrial waste, the actor turned to the camera as a tear falls slowly from one eye.

Viewers were invited to relieve their guilt by taking action against pollution. To gain support for restrictions on oil pumping in coastal areas, activists might outrage the public with pictures of sea birds coated in oil spilled by drilling rigs. Recently, activists have used fear-based appeals to warn of the dangers of bio-engineered crops, emphasizing that the potential health consequences of such plants are unknown and potentially dire.

The talk-show hosts and news anchors who populate cable television attract and retain audiences by continually stoking their sense of moral outrage. In the US, this is particularly evident on obviously partisan "news" networks, such as Fox News or MSNBC. Here the hosts spent much of their time highlighting misdeeds of opposing politicians; questioning the character of whole groups of people ("liberals," "conservatives"); offering a steady stream of sarcastic, mocking commentary; and generally working the audience into a righteous lather of indignation. The result is an apparent emotional connection between host and audience, one designed to keep reviewers returning for more affirmation of their own moral superiority. The emotional temperature gradually rises over the course of the show, as the host deftly "reveals" the latest scheming, hypocritical, and shameful practices of the opposition and the audience is left in headshaking disbelief at the moral inferiority of those in the "wrong" political or cultural camp. For cable television hosts, ratings are apparently driven by the heat of emotional warfare rather than by calm and collegial argument.

Politicians also play on moral emotions. They call on their followers to be courageous, routinely characterize their opponents as spineless, and champion themselves as fearless agents of reform. Based on their campaign advertisements, American politicians are apparently ashamed of their government but deeply proud of their country. They may be appalled by the lax moral standards of society even as they are indignant about government efforts to regulate private behavior. The politician who raises fears about the dangers of immigration may also express dread when regulations are imposed on the hiring of illegal workers. The candidate who expresses remorse over past mistakes is unsympathetic to the mistakes of opponents. These apparently contradictory messages reveal the emotional dexterity of political occupations. The emotions cultivated by politicians are adapted to varying audiences and calibrated to the place and time of an appearance. The emotional labor of political life is complicated. Audiences will mistrust the candidate who changes emotional gears too often, perhaps viewing him or her as inauthentic or morally suspect. The politician who lacks emotional zeal in prosecuting her opponents could fail to motivate the voters and become a victim of poor election turnout. Those who are perceived to be insensitive to the hardships of citizens, or overly sensitive when criticized themselves, may be judged as too "cold" or "touchy." All of these responses suggest that political survival requires striking the right emotional cords, with deftly crafted moral messages. That is no easy job.

Emotional Utility Players

The employees I label "emotional utility players" are adept at performing emotional communication tasks that underlay any number of jobs. Typically, it is not their occupation that compels them to perform this work, although they may perform any number of the jobs described above. Rather, these employees perform valuable emotional functions for their organizations or workgroups, over and above their required job duties. They do it informally.

Toxin Handlers

Toxin handling is one such function (Frost, 2003). These employees are adept at managing the emotions that can have a poisoning effect on organizational relationships and performance. Elena, who works in the community education department of a large hospital, played the part of toxin handler, calming her boss down until the situation blew over:

A new co-worker was overwhelmed by his job and actually forgot to attend one of our weekend events. He was confused about the schedule. My boss was livid, because we were shorthanded. On Monday, she reamed him, yelling and threatening to fire him. I heard it all and thought it was unfair. I wasn't sure what to do, but I was upset about the poor treatment. I decided to let her calm down and then talked to her privately. I told her I understood her anger, but the new guy wasn't really at fault. He didn't know he was "just expected" to be at every event. She seemed calmer and eventually apologized to him. The situation blew over. We have all been working together ever since, with no big problems. I think my boss knows she overreacted and I did the right thing. (Waldron and Kassing, 2011: 1)

Other examples are familiar. Consider the team leader who provides a more optimistic counter-narrative to the always gloomy prognostications of an embittered member. Think about the intrepid peer who speaks up in defense of a co-worker who has experienced humiliation at the hands of an office bully. As has been noted previously, toxin handlers can be organizational heroes but they pay a price for their emotional exertions (Frost and Robinson, 1999). Handling the emotional baggage of others can be risky and exhausting.

Mood shifters

Mood-shifting is another emotional function. For our purposes, a mood is a generalized feeling shared by organizational members over a period of time (also see Planalp, 1999). Moods often have no one cause or point of reference; the workgroup may be in a happy or apprehensive mood, but the cause of the mood is typically not a single action, person, or event. Mood shifters know how to "lighten the mood," often by offering timely and humorous observations. They alter the mood by noting the absurd or unfamiliar circumstances that are feeding it ("Well, Toto, this isn't Kansas anymore!"). Mood shifters also use temporal framing to orient co-workers toward the emotional possibilities of the future. "Look," they might say to dispirited co-workers, "this is a bad situation, but if we work hard and stay together things will get better." The result might be a more hopeful mood.

91

Emotion articulators

Articulating emotion is a third role played by these employees, some of whom are gifted in the art of matching feelings with words and language. They help co-workers fine-tune their emotional expressions. The author once overheard two co-workers trying to reconcile after a heated and hurtful exchange during a faculty meeting. "I wish the argument had not been so personal," said the most offensive of the disputants. A third faculty member, who had observed the dispute, offered an interpretation: "So maybe [name] is saying that he feels some *remorse* over his choice of words." The offender nodded his head in response and the parties seemed to relax a bit. The observer had found just the right emotional label.

Emotion articulators help their peers learn that what they are feeling is "justifiable outrage," "emotional shell shock," "power envy," or a host of other emotional reactions. In this sense, they are the informal mental health counselors of the workplace, helping workers make better sense of feelings and their possible causes. Of course, in some cases, these interpretations are expressions of cultural or managerial bias. When a leader suggests that a female employee lacks "humility," the message may be simply reinforcing the organization's patriarchic preferences. Perhaps a male employee exhibiting similar emotional behavior would be described with organizationally legitimate labels, such as "bold" or "confident."

I should note that the informal emotional contributions made by utility players overlap with the formal tasks performed by occupational specialists. After all, human resource officers are trained to manage a variety of emotionally toxic situations. Internal communication specialists may see it as their job to create messages that manage the moods of the workforce. And some people actually are mental health counselors and they do help employees articulate their emotions. Nonetheless, much of this emotional labor is the intangible contribution of non-specialists, many of whom are valued because they are "good with people," no matter what their "real job" may happen to be.

Occupational Socialization: Learning the Emotional Ropes

Before leaving our discussion of emotional occupations, we take up briefly the topic of occupational socialization. How do workers come to understand the emotional requirements of various types of work? As any member of a family knows, emotional communication practices are consequential long before we enter the workplace. Learning to communicate emotion appropriately is a fundamental task of childhood. Parents spend considerable effort to control the feelings expressed by their children – and, just as important, themselves. Later, experiences at school refine these emotional expectations and lay the foundation for the nuanced communication of feelings that is central to so many contemporary occupations. All of this happens within a larger cultural milieu, where children and adults are exposed to the emotional performances associated with various kinds of work. Some of this socialization is mediated, as when television shows feature the (often unrealistic) emotional lives of police officers or nurses, secretaries or stay-at-home parents. The exposure is more direct when children observe the emotional practices of the workers who surround them – sports coaches, religious leaders, parents of friends, adult relatives. In this section, we consider just a few of the more potent sources of occupational socialization (for a thorough review, see Kramer, 2010).

Parenting and family experiences

Parents often teach their children the emotional communication competencies that they will need in the workplace, encouraging them to "use their words" to express feelings while modeling emotional communication ("Daddy feels frustrated right now and he needs some time alone"). Children learn to be empathetic and compassionate when parents encourage them to consider the emotional reactions of people and media characters. About playground behavior they might ask, "How do you think that boy felt when his friends left him out of the game?" About a violent act witnessed on television: "In real life, how would it feel to be hit like that? How would his mother or father feel if he was hurt and had to go to the hospital?" At the same time, emotional hardiness might be encouraged: "it is normal to feel sad when someone dies. Even though we are sad, Grandma would want us to go back to our work and school, and do our best."

In contrast, employees may have been raised in families that veiled, discouraged, or even punished expressions of emotion. Children might be mocked or even physically punished for crying; emotional displays may be considered signs of weakness. In others families, tantrums and emotional aggression are tolerated or rewarded, leaving children with the impression that emotion can be used for manipulative purposes. These childhood influences may be muted over time, but echoes of them are often observed at work. Shawna, a sales person at a small medical supply company, shared this anecdote, which concerned the business manager.

> She is kind of controlling. Even the tiniest little transaction needs to be approved by her. I'm serious! If I want a pencil out of the supply cabinet, she needs to approve. Anyway, due to her micromanaging personality, all of these requests pile up and she gets more and more stressed out. We are waiting for her and getting impatient because we can't do our jobs. Typically this results in a meltdown on her end, with her sending nasty emails and pouting like a child who needs a nap. A lot of us are getting tired of her act!

Childhood activities

Another source of emotional socialization training is the social and recreational activities that defined our childhood. Many of today's workers learned their work preferences through a highly regimented set of developmental experiences, all of which social-ized them to feel and express emotion in particular ways. A short list might include youth sports, ballet lessons, girl scouts, computer camps, faith-based group activities, and theatrical performances. These activities have many purposes, but among those listed by parents are those with emotional themes. For example, the parents of a high-school football player told me that a key reason for playing the sport was to develop courage and emotional toughness. The mother of a veteran (14-year-old) gymnast described the poise developed by her daughter, who faced even the most harrowing of balance-beam routines with a remarkable sense of calm.

When the author's youngest child launched a short-lived soccer "career" at the age of five, he was startled by the emotional education provided by screeching parents who during the very first game lurched madly up and down the sidelines, following the antics of the confused but tireless midgets running randomly around the field. "Show more aggression!" "Stop laughing and get moving!," and "No tears allowed!" These messages foreshadowed a season-long fusillade of emotion-shaping directives. Even these very young players modeled the emotional performances of their sports heroes, which they had witnessed on television. When the referee blew a whistle to signal an infraction (or failed to do so) players threw up their hands in exasperation, adopted deeply pained facial grimaces, and sometimes even rolled on the ground in feigned expressions of agony. These child athletes were quickly adopting the emotional communication practices that would, in their parents' eyes, serve them well as they faced the competitive and cooperative pressures of the adult world. Having observed some of these athletes as they progressed into adulthood, we find it no stretch to claim that the emotional character of some employees may be foreshadowed by the sideline antics of their emotional parents, so many years before.

Participation in sport can provide children with social, emotional, and health benefits. But, as other researchers have observed, many American youth end their involvement in organized sports prematurely, due in part to the emotionally draining nature of their relationships with parents, coaches, and "fans" (Meân and Kassing, 2008). In the US, this may be due to the hyper-competitive and increasingly professionalized nature of sport. Competition is a central cultural value in the US and a defining feature of its capitalistic economy, so it is not surprising that many parents involve their children in competitive sports. Competition can generate excitement and motivate athletes to improve their skills. At its best, youth sport teaches important emotional lessons that should translate, eventually, to the workplace – the pride that comes with accomplishment, the joy of teamwork, the emotional resilience required in times of adversity, the graceful response to winning and losing, and the poise one needs to perform under pressure in front of an audience (see Kassing and Barber, 2007).

Media modeling

Television and popular films are other sources of occupational socialization (Kramer, 2010). By watching their favorite shows, the public may form expectations about the "normal" emotional communication practices of detectives, nurses, or teachers. Of course, certain occupations are highly overrepresented in prime television, in part because the work itself can be emotionally riveting. That is why so many hours of television are devoted to murder investigations, the drama and trauma of the hospital emergency room, and high-speed police pursuits. But the work of most occupations goes unnoticed on television, and the real-life labors of police officers and doctors are more likely to be routine than dramatic. On TV, the emotional behaviors of TV workers is likely to reflect gender and cultural stereotypes. All of this leads to the conclusion that prospective workers learn relatively little useful information from popular media about the emotional requirements of various career paths. The information that is learned is likely to be distorted, leaving new workers unprepared for the emotional requirements of their chosen professions.

Formal education and training

Workers can gain some degree of emotional savvy from formal schooling. For example, classes in organizational communication, industrial psychology, and human resources management may include formal instruction on emotional communication practices, such as conflict management or the delivery of constructive criticism. Occupation-specific learning may be provided in the form of case studies or guest presentations by workers. Some academic disciplines have come to recognize that students must be better prepared for the emotional rigors of their professions. In response to high dropout rates, teacher-training programs may provide students with more supervised experience in the classroom and also provide increased assistance for seasoned teachers. Internship programs and extended service learning experiences may help students better understand the emotional requirements of various occupations.

As with the Disney company (mentioned above), organizations expend considerable resources in preparing workers for the emotional demands of work, particularly service work. Instruction on such topics "as keeping the customer happy" and "dealing with difficult people" are examples. So too is training in recognizing the "warning signs" of overstressed employees, emotionally distraught patients, or fearful airline passengers. As discussed in chapter 1, some companies have invested heavily in increasing the emotional competence of current or future workers. These training programs underscore the importance of emotional communication in so many professions. They also suggest that those who prepare themselves for the emotional side of work are more likely to be successful in at least some occupations.

Diverse life experiences

Early life experiences may socialize employees to be more emotionally discerning, empathetic, and resilient. For example, when they travel abroad, US citizens are sometimes surprised by the feelings of resentment they encounter among citizens of some countries and expressions of admiration by others. Of course, relationships with other countries are multifaceted, so a mix of emotional responses might be encountered. This nuanced discernment of emotion may be valuable at work, where mixed feelings often prevail. If they invest the effort to understand these different and complex emotional reactions, travelers broaden their empathetic capacity. Given the likelihood that employees will encounter co-workers and customers from various cultures, this form of empathy is an invaluable asset in many occupations. Finally, employees who have experienced hardships and persevered may be more emotionally resilient than those who have yet to be tested.

Conclusion

We attempted in this chapter to provide a representative sampling of the many and diverse occupations in which the communication of emotion is an essential requirement. Unfortunately, we lack the space to cover all of the relevant occupations in detail, or even all of the most interesting ones. Readers can find detailed occupational studies elsewhere, including those of sex workers (Sanders, 2005), funeral directors (Smith, Dorsey, and Mosley, 2009), or detectives (Jackall, 2000). We should add that emotional experiences are so ubiquitous that nearly any job calls for it to be communicated, or at least suppressed, to some degree. In this chapter, we focused on jobs where emotional performances are complicated, embedded in the work role, and impactful. We paid less attention to those professions that have received considerable attention elsewhere, in part because the emotional performance is so obvious to the public. Sales clerks and police officers are two such examples.

Nonetheless, the examples provided in this chapter demonstrate that emotion is integral to the performance of many kinds of work. Although the jobs vary tremendously, several emotional communication tasks were important across professions. One of those tasks is using communication to cue audiences to feel emotions that otherwise might not be experienced. We see this in the stand-up comedian who uses narrative and comedic timing to cue her audience to laugh, or the talk-show host who uses sarcasm to humiliate guests and provoke outrage. A second task involves emotional instruction. Dr Phil is an example as he frequently explains the emotions that his guests must learn to feel. Drill sergeants are teachers too, as they prepare soldiers for the emotions they will experience (or manage) during war. Emotional boundary workers regulate the flow of emotion, a third task. These jobs require the employee to monitor, absorb, and label feelings that flow between visitors and co-workers.

In a fourth task, communication and emotion are connected through rituals, which create meaning through structured, repeated, emotional experiences that are shared with other people in similar circumstances. We used the label "sacred seekers" to describe those workers who design experiences that help followers enrich their emotional lives. Coaches fashion season-long emotional game plans, which often include ritualized experiences like emotion-charging pre-game huddles and half-time pep talks. Funeral directors also fit this category. We identify deep acting as a distinctive fifth emotional communication task, one in which workers come to genuinely feel the emotions that are demanded by their work. Interestingly, ritual also facilitates deep acting, as we saw in the case of Dan, the highly committed salesperson who participated in a ritualized training before launching his summer-long career as a bookseller. Ritual was also important to hospice workers as they used a weekly gathering to stay in touch with the grief and compassion required by their very important jobs. Finally, we identified the "cooling-out" occupations, in which the communication task is to calm existing emotions. In their very different ways, crisis workers and con artists illustrated this interesting sixth form of emotional communication.

As we noted in chapter 2, communication is a complex phenomenon. It expresses and shapes workplace emotion though cultural practices, collective performances, organizational narratives, language, non-verbal cues, interaction patterns, and the tactics used by individual employees. The process of learning an occupation is also complex, but these elements of emotional communication are central (and sometimes unrecognized) components of the socialization process. We learn about the emotional requirements of occupations though media depictions, schooling, family influences, training, and interactions with co-workers. In these contexts, communication is the means by which our understandings of workplace emotions are formed. But, as we have observed in this chapter, communication is also the means by which emotion is expressed, in so many different ways, once we are on the job.

References

Carey, B. (2009). Mental stress training is planned for U.S. soldiers (August 15). Retrieved from: <http://www.nytimes.com/2009/08/18/health/18psych.html>.

CBS News (2007). Texting while driving (September). Retrieved from YouTube. com: <http://www.youtube.com/watch?v=fDlYSPVro0Q>.

Frost, P. J. (2003). *Toxic Emotions at Work.* Cambridge, MA: Harvard Business School Press.

Frost, P. J., and Robinson, S. (1999). The toxin handler: organization hero and Casualty. *Harvard Business Review* (July–August): 96–106.

Gallup Organization (2010). *Mississippians Go to Church the Most; Vermonters, Least* (February 1). Retrieved from Gallup.com: <http://www.gallup.com/poll/125999/Mississippians-Go-Church-Most-Vermonters- Least.aspx>.

Goffman, E. G. (1952). On cooling the mark out: some aspects of adaptation to failure. *Psychiatry*, 15: 451–63.

Harlos, K. P., and Pinder, C. C. (2000). Emotion and injustice in the workplace. In S. Fineman (ed.), *Emotion in Organizations* (2nd edn). London, Sage, pp. 255–76.

Henson, L., and Parameswaran, R. (2008). Getting real with "tell it like it is" talk therapy: hegemonic masculinity and the *Dr. Phil* show. *Communication: Culture and Critique*, 1: 287–310.

Hochschild, A. (1983). *The Managed Heart.* Berkeley, CA: University of California Press.

Jackall, R. (2000). A detective's lot: contours of morality and emotion in police work. In S. Fineman (ed.), *Emotion in Organizations* (2nd edn). London, Sage, pp. 227–40.

Kassing, J., and Barber, A. (2007). Being a good sport: an investigation of sportsmanship messages provided by youth soccer parents, officials, and coaches. *Human Communication*, 10: 61–8.

Katz, N. (2009). Sweat lodge death investigation turns to self-help guru James Arthur Ray (October). Retrieved May 17, 2010, from CBS News.com: <http://www.cbsnews.com/8301-504083_162-5378668-504083.html>.

Kidwell, M. (2006). "Calm down!": the role of gaze in the interactional management of hysteria by the police. *Discourse Studies*, 8: 745–70.

Klass, P. (1987). *A Not Entirely Benign Procedure: Four Years as a Medical Student.* New York: G. P. Putnam.

Klass, P. (2007). *Treatment Kind and Fair: Letters to a Young Doctor.* New York: Basic Books.

Kramer, M. (2010). *Organizational Socialization: Joining and Leaving Organizations.* Cambridge: Polity.

Meân, L., and Kassing, J. (2008). Identities at youth sporting events: a critical discourse analysis. *International Journal of Sport Communication*, 1: 42–66.

Pauley, B. (2010). How to perform your standup routine at school [interviewed by Christian Thom]. Retrieved from the *Comedy Insider* website: <http://www. wonderhowto.com/how-to-perform-stand-comedy-routine-school-184357/>.

Prescott, R. M. K. (2002). [Rhona Marie Knox Prescott interviewed by J. Kent]. *Experiencing War: Stories from the Veterans' History Project*. Retrieved from Library of Congress: <http://lcweb2.loc.gov/diglib/vhp-stories/loc.natlib. afc2001001.01146/>.

Prus, R. (1989). *Making Sales: Influence as Interpersonal Accomplishment*. Newbury Park, CA: Sage.

Running, A., Woodward, L., and Girard, D. (2008). Ritual: the final expression of care. *International Journal of Nursing Practice*, 14: 303–7.

Sanders, T. (2005). "It's just acting": sex workers' strategies for capitalizing on sexuality. *Gender, Work, and Organization*, 12: 319–42.

Smith, J. R., Dorsey, K. D., and Mosley, A. L. (2009). Licensed funeral directors: an empirical analysis of the dimensions and consequences of emotional labor. *International Management Review*, 5: 30–44.

Sutton, R. I., and Rafaeli, A. (1988). Untangling the relationship between displayed emotions and organizational sales: the case of convenience stores. *Academy of Management Journal*, 31: 461–87.

Tracy, S. J., and Tracy, K. (1998). Emotion labor at 911: a case study and theoretical critique. *Journal of Applied Communication Research*, 26: 390–411.

United States Bureau of Labor Statistics (2008). *Occupational Employment Statistics*. Retrieved from; <http://data.bls.gov:8080/oes/search.jsp>.

Waldron, V. (1994). Once more, *with feeling*. Reconsidering the role of emotion in work. In S. Deitz (ed.), *Communication Yearbook 17*, New York: Lawrence Erlbaum Publishers, pp. 388–416.

Waldron, V. (2000). Relational experiences and emotion at work. In S. Fineman (ed.), *Emotion in Organizations* (2nd edn). London, Sage, pp. 64–82.

Waldron, V., and Kassing, J. K. (2011). *Managing Risk in Communication Encounters*. Thousand Oaks, CA: Sage.

Waldron, V., and Krone, K. J. (1991). The experience and expression of emotion in the workplace: a study of a corrections organization. *Management Communication Quarterly*, 4: 287–309.

Wilson, T. R. (1996). The sources of true motivation in football coaching. *Coach and Athletic Director* (February). Retrieved from: <http://www.allbusiness. com/human-resources/workforce-management/576877-1.html>.

4

Work Relationships

Getting Emotional with Peers, Supervisors, and Others

Help! My boss keeps putting me down.

Dear Annie: I was hired about three months ago as part of a 12-person training team, and I really like the job and my colleagues, with one exception. Our team leader can't seem to stop picking people apart and tearing down everything we do, even when we have followed his requests to the letter. He's an incredibly negative person – the glass is always more than half empty – which unfortunately is contagious. Morale here is in the dumps, with everyone just going through the motions.

At first I lost sleep over his snide comments and went out of my way to try harder to please him, to no avail. So lately I find myself just trying to stay out of his way and avoid him altogether, but it's not always practical. (This is also the approach several of my teammates take.) I'm looking for a job in a different part of the company, but if I don't manage to escape for a while, is there anything I can do about his constant carping?

Color Me Blue

As "Color Me Blue" reveals in this post to a work advice website (Fisher, 2010), relationships with other people are often the source of positive and negative workplace emotions. For many employees, leader–member relationships are the source of intense feelings. These can spread across the larger network of employees. In this case, the relentlessly negative boss, with his penchant for "picking people apart," is apparently the source of pervasive feelings of low morale. As often happens in workgroups, these feelings have coalesced into a mood, an atmosphere of dispiritedness. Admirably, Color Me Blue has tried to rectify the situation using a variety of emotion-management strategies. First, she tried conscientious compliance with her boss's wishes in an effort to keep him happy. Then she tried to avoid him. Now, having already lost some sleep over these relational stresses, she is looking for a more positive boss, or at least one that is less emotionally toxic. In essence, Color Me Blue has been forced to detach herself emotionally from her supervisor, even as she must remain engaged in her work.

As was suggested in chapter 3, many workers perform emotionally demanding tasks. Think about the work of emergency-room nurses, police officers, or nursery school teachers. But in my own analyses of emotional narratives I have noticed that *relationships* with co-workers, not tasks, are the most commonly cited source of intense feelings. Participants in one of the earliest studies were probation officers (Waldron and Krone, 1991). They interacted every day with hardened criminals who had recently been released from prison. The officers monitored their charges closely, sometimes tracking them down in rough neighborhoods and enforcing compliance with parole requirements. Although their tasks exposed them to potentially dangerous people and tense confrontations, it was not the work itself that the probation officers found to be emotional. Instead, they described intense encounters with supervisors and co-workers. In anonymous surveys, they detailed painful episodes of public embarrassment at the hands of highly critical bosses; powerful rage directed at "backstabbing" peers; and deep disgust at what they considered to be abusive managers.

For this reason, chapter 4 explores work relationships as important sites of emotional interaction. I discuss the unique qualities of work relationships and then consider the role of emotional communication in maintaining, building, damaging, and repairing relationships between members and leaders. I look at the special emotional freedoms and responsibilities enjoyed by powerful people. Peer relationships are considered next – the difficult ones and the rewarding ones. The special emotional challenges of workplace romances and "blended" (co-worker/friend relationships) are also explored, and I examine how emotion travels across the boundaries of work and family relationships, considering, for example, how family life can buffer or exacerbate the emotional stresses of the workplace.

Work Relationships are Emotionally Unique

All interpersonal relationships are sites for emotional communication. Whenever people are connected by bonds of caring, whenever they closely coordinate their efforts to achieve important goals, their interactions have the potential to become emotional. However, workplace bonds are "emotionally unique" in at least five ways. The first of these involves risk; these are often high-stakes relationships. Their success or failure affects our incomes, careers, and the degree to which our daily experiences at work are rewarding, mundane, or miserable. For that reason, employees may feel increased pressure to strike the right emotional key in their interactions with clients, peers, or supervisors. After all, many relationships are involuntary. We *have to* maintain them. The process starts with the selection interview, where emotional effervescence is required. Was your previous employer beastly? Your job search exasperating? No matter. All traces of bitterness must be banished in an effort to make an emotional connection with the interviewer, in the hope of making a long-term connection with the organization. Once hired, the stakes are high in other key conversations with workplace partners, all of whom will be forming impressions based on emotional displays. How will the rookie employee hold up during her first encounter with an angry client? How will he react to negative feedback during that first performance review? When asked to make an important presentation on behalf of her work team, will she reveal feelings of confidence or trepidation? In short, employees' emotional performances with clients, supervisors, and peers can enhance their chances for career advancement or put them at risk.

A second unique factor in work relationships is status inequality. Employees often find themselves in interactions with people who are more or less powerful. Given this reality, it is no surprise that certain kinds of work interaction are tinged with the emotion of fear. For fear of the consequences, employees are sometimes reluctant to be the bearers of bad news (Rosen and Tesser, 1970; Wagoner and Waldron, 1999). In some cases, this wariness is quite justified. As I have noted previously, "fear, frustration, and rage often appear in narratives about supervisory abuses of power. Hopeless despair or burning indignation may be the emotional reaction to repeated and persistent misuses of power" (Waldron, 2009: 13). But trepidation is also felt by some supervisors, who hesitate to deliver corrective feedback for fear that it will cause an emotional blow-up or harm valued relationships (Larson, 1989).

Emotional communication plays an integral role in efforts to gain, keep, or undermine power. Members may decide to humble an arrogant team leader by playing a practical joke or staging a coordinated work delay (Waldron, 2000). In some organizations, workers are cautious not to appear *excessively proud* after promotions for fear that less successful peers will interpret their behavior as gloating (Waldron and Krone, 1991). In contrast, others may flatter powerful people in an effort to cultivate good feelings. These efforts at emotional manipulation are sometimes belittled by peers who describe it with terms like "ass kissing," "self pimping," or "slobbering."

Workplace encounters are often conducted in public. Co-workers and clients may serve as witnesses to some of our more emotional moments, and it may be their presence that makes them emotional in the first place. This is the third way that work relationships are emotionally unique. The audience heightens our chances of feeling such emotions as pride, embarrassment, or shame. Indeed, in workplace narratives that I collect for my research, employees indicate that the public nature of some interaction is what makes them emotionally intense. That was certainly the case with Louis, who worked as a short-order cook in a busy restaurant.

One evening, right in the middle of the dinner rush, the floor manager stormed through the doors of the kitchen. His face was red and his eyes were all bulging out and he was waving a plate of food in the air, which he brought right up to my face. He was yelling and looking at me. "Who let a hair fall on to this plate!" A customer had been grossed out by the hair and left the restaurant. My boss thought it was my hair, but that was impossible. I wore a hair net and it wasn't even my color. The other cooks all stood back and looked at me and the waitresses were all gawking at me through the pick-up window. It was pretty much the most humiliating experience of my life.

Louis' feelings may be compounded as he realizes that his encounter with the angry boss is being re-enacted as various informal accounts are passed through along the informal communication network. Employees who were absent on the day of the original event will hear about it when they return to work. They in turn will bring the story home and pass it on to family and friends, some of whom know Louis. The boss's emotional outburst, perhaps even more than the errant hair, will be the "juiciest" part of the story. Astonishment. Horror. Sympathy. Glee. These and other emotional responses will be attached to the account as it passes through the ranks. It may circle back to Louis, as employees seek him out to verify the facts or express their sympathy. In this way, he will be reminded of the emotional event even as the experience is recolored by the sentiment of his peers and the passing of time. In these ways, employees experience *second-order* emotions. These feelings are echoes of those felt during the original encounter, filtered through a rippling series of conversations. In this sense, organizational emotion is not only attributable to the presence of an audience; it is also *reproduced* through the interactions of the audience.

A fourth unique feature of organizational relationships is their connection to task performance. In many kinds of labor, co-workers must work interdependently. Successful experiences of cooperation can forge emotional bonds among workers. These are strongest when workers depend on each other for safety and survival. For example, soldiers develop intense emotional commitments to comrades who "watch their backs." Similar feelings can develop among other workers who labor collectively to ward off danger – firefighters, crews on deep-sea fishing boats, and construction workers who scale the heights to build skyscrapers or dams. In these professions, emotional communication among co-workers serves such functions as managing fear, building feelings of camaraderie, and, sometimes, expressing feelings of grief.

Of course, most workers perform less harrowing tasks. But even mundane forms of task interdependence yield emotional responses. Who has not experienced the pride that comes from successful teamwork or intense frustration at members who failed to carry their weight? In addition to triggering emotional reactions, task-related interactions provide guidance about appropriate forms of emotional expression. For example, if workers' facial expressions reveal disgust for an unpleasant task, they may be reminded of their emotional responsibilities with comments such as "Hey, it's show time," or "Get your game face on," or "Don't let it get you down."

The production of emotion is the object of some collective forms of work. I noticed this when observing the behaviors of courtroom judges, defense attorneys, and prosecutors (Waldron, 2000). They appeared to work collaboratively to create feelings of dread in the juvenile delinquents who often appeared before the court, perhaps in the hope of "scaring them straight." The defense and prosecuting attorneys cooperated in a "good cop/bad cop" routine, apparently designed to make the defendants feel relief and gratitude when they received probation rather than jail time. Similarly collaborative forms of emotional labor are observed when pilots and crew work together to calm frightened airline passengers after a bout of turbulence, or a troupe of street performers works to surprise and then delight their audience.

A final emotionally unique feature of work relationships is, interestingly enough, their tendency to affect our lives outside of work. Employees often can't help but bring home with them the joys and disappointments they experience at work. However,

recognizing that any type of communal arrangement requires some degree of emotional constraint, workers strive to "keep things under control," to "put a lid on it," even on the most trying of days. Unedited venting and emotional exhaustion may be the unattractive alternatives to this collective attempt at emotional censorship. Emotions repressed at work, however, are sometimes displaced. At home, family members may become the unwitting targets of suppressed anger ... Family members are usually safer audiences for expressions of envy at co-workers, fear of abusive supervisors, and indignation over unjust practices. However, habitual displacement may lead to emotional fatigue among family members and supportive friends. They may learn to carefully edit work-related discussions, so as to avoid another round of emotional dumping. (Waldron, 2009: 14)

It is not just emotion that flows across the permeable boundaries of organizations. In some cases, the relationship itself is a kind of bridge between the professional and personal realms. This happens when co-workers are also friends, an arrangement that researchers call a "blended" relationship (Bridge and Baxter, 1992). Workplace romance is another example. And, complicating things even further, are those examples of family businesses in which co-workers may also be spouses, children, or relatives. These unique cases make the larger point – emotional communication can't be easily compartmentalized "within" workplace relationships.

Workplace varieties of relational emotion

In a general sense, most emotions are "relational" because they arise from interactions with other people or systems created by people. But in the stories I have collected over the years, a relatively small set of emotions are invoked to characterize relationships with co-workers. Table 4.1 presents some of these. Those with positive connotations include admiration, pride, and affection. However, encounters with co-workers also yield envy, guilt, and shame.

Types of Work Relationships

Although many of the emotional requirements of work are dictated by the norms of organizational culture and the larger society,

Table 4.1 Emotional descriptions of work relationships

Emotion/feeling	Discourse example
Admiration	She would do anything for us employees. I felt admiration for her.
Camaraderie	"We were comrades in arms. The feeling of connection was intense."
Compassion	"Kindness. We were like a work family that cared for each other."
Envy	"I wanted, she got the promotion that I really deserved."
Guilt	"I felt guilty leaving my co-workers; we went through so much together."
Jealousy	"Basically, the boss and I got along great, which made my peers jealous."
Joy/happiness	". . . delightful place to work; I couldn't have been happier with the people."
Love/affection	"I liked my "cube mate" so much that I ended up marrying him!"
Loneliness	"I missed my old co-workers. The new job was lonely."
Pride	". . . proud of our team effort. It was crazy but we served every customer."
Shame	"I will never forget how he humiliated me in front of all my co-workers."

they do vary across relationship types. The most prominent types are explored below.

Leaders and followers

Many work relationships require members to meet the requirements of leadership or followership. And, of course, some employees play the role of leader in some relationships and follower in others. Leader–member relationships are defined most notably by differences in status. Status originates from a variety of sources: a designated leadership role, seniority, technical expertise, and so on. In some cases, leaders are informal or quasi-formal, as when a senior employee serves as an unofficial mentor for a newcomer or an expert teacher agrees to "coach" her less accomplished colleagues. Despite these variations, emotional communication is always integral to the performance of leadership and followership.

Emotional qualities of leadership: Leadership takes many forms, all of which have been examined elsewhere in great detail (for an accessible review, see Northhouse, 2010). However, most leadership definitions include some reference to emotion. Transformational leaders are known for inspiring followers to exceed expectations and for inviting them to make radical changes in their values and aspirations (Bass and Riggio, 2006). Unlike transactional leadership approaches, which view leadership as an exchange of resources (e.g., recognition, money, effort) between leader and member, the transformational approach focuses on the emotions and developmental potential of workers.

A variety of related forms of leadership has evolved from this concept. Emotion is perhaps most implicated in the performance of *charismatic* leaders, who are known for their ability to make emotional connections with followers (Conger, 1999). They do so through the use of passionate, values-focused rhetoric; by making appeals to emotions such as pride, fear, or disgust; or by setting an emotionally resonant personal example. This form of leadership is sometimes associated with the American president Ronald Reagan, who frequently invoked values such as freedom and independence in his speeches and urged citizens to feel pride in American exceptionalism. Reagan was portrayed as unfailingly optimistic and cheerful.

Negative examples of charismatic leadership abound, with the most obvious being Adolph Hitler, the German leader who roused extreme feelings of disgust in a downtrodden citizenry. He did so with the technique of scapegoating, blaming whole classes of "inferior" people for Germany's problems – Jews, homosexuals, gypsies. In this case, the consequences of emotion-driven leadership were horrible and deadly. An obvious concern with charismatic leadership is its potential to motivate unethical behavior. In fact, unethical charismatic leaders may encourage followers to ignore "moral emotions," like guilt and humility (Haidt 2003; see also chapter 5), which might guide them to responsible behavior. Indeed, leadership ethicist Jill Graham (1995) warned that organizational citizens sometimes sacrifice reason and moral principles in their zealous pursuit of a charismatic leader's vision. Even the charismatic Reagan was prone to scapegoating, as he sometimes blamed "welfare mothers" for his nation's economic ills.

In response to the potential abuses of charismatic leadership, several alternatives have been proposed. *Servant* leaders are inspirational, but they also express humility in their efforts to do what is best for their followers and communities (Graham, 1991). More recently, the notion of *authentic* leadership has been developing in the literature (Gardner, Avolio, Luthans, May, and Walumbwa, 2005; George, 2003). Authentic leaders are thought to be self-aware, transparent, morally responsible, and, of course, heartfelt. Their life stories often include triumph over hardship or tragedy. Emotionally, authentic leaders are said to be positive, hopeful, and resilient. Presumably, followers find leaders to be authentic based in part on the display of authentic-seeming emotion.

From even this brief discussion, it is clear that emotional communication is an important component of leadership, for better or for worse. As the research evolves, theorists are becoming more guarded about the role of emotion in leadership ethics. Rather than focus exclusively on convincing emotional performances, they seem to be viewing emotion as an indicator of the shared humanity of leader and follower. Indeed, as leadership becomes more of a shared responsibility in our decentralized organizations, this trend is likely to accelerate.

Emotional qualities of followership: The emotional requirements of followership have received less attention in the research literature, although the emotional communication competencies discussed in chapter 1 certainly apply here. I would add several other qualities. One is *hardiness*, the capacity to 'bear up" under the emotional demands of work. Hardy followers can persevere through periods of emotional turbulence and stress and they are able to outlast leaders who are emotionally abusive or unstable. A related concept, emotional *resilience,* extends beyond mere perseverance (for a detailed discussion, see Buzzanell, Shenoy, Remke, and Lucas, 2009). Resilient people make constructive adjustments in reaction to disruptive experiences. But they also find positive emotional experiences in work. Over long periods of time, they seem to thrive and flourish. Resilient followers are hopeful, optimistic, and emotionally flexible. Regarding this last characteristic, these employees are quick to abandon emotions such as despair. They take actions that produce emotions like admiration, hope, and satisfaction: building new relationships with respected peers, devising promising plans for the future, or focusing more intensely on fulfilling aspects of their work. A fourth quality, *selective emotional engagement*, is suggested by the work of organizational communication researcher Sarah Tracy (2009), who argues that emotionally savvy employees learn to manage stress by recalibrating their emotional involvement in work relationships and tasks. So, for example, if interactions with a difficult supervisor become too emotionally draining, they engage more intensively with mentors or peers or with non-work friends.

In recent years, scholars have begun to conceptualize the role of follower as a complex and important social identity (e.g., Collinson, 2006). Indeed, following well may be as emotionally demanding as leading well and, like leadership, followership can take a variety of forms. In a qualitative interview study of 31 lower- and mid-level employees drawn from a variety of industries, researchers examined the meanings associated with followership (Carsten, Uhl-Bien, West, Patera, and McGregor, 2010). The respondents described three different types of followers: passive, active, and proactive. In emotional terms, *passive* followers experience humility. They are obedient, emotionally reticent, and relieved that leaders are willing and able to bear the emotional stresses that come with responsibility. *Active* followers are more likely to express their feelings to leaders, although they too believe it is important to conform to leader expectations. They show little fear of speaking up. *Proactive* followers view themselves as "co-leaders." They assume some of the emotional responsibilities of leadership, assuming that it is part of their job to deflect or absorb the emotions that might otherwise be directed at leaders. For example, they might intervene to resolve a heated dispute among colleagues without consulting the leader and without fear of reprisal. Active and proactive followers seemed to welcome emotional aspects of work, as indicated by this quotation from an active follower, who participated in the study:

> I don't care for people who sit there and just say, "I don't know, it wasn't my decision, I'm just following." I don't mind taking the buck if I know why, and let people get angry at me if they are not happy. (Carsten et al., 2010: 553)

Power, status, and autonomy   Team leaders, managers, and heads of organizations enjoy a status advantage in their relationships with less powerful co-workers. From an emotional communication perspective, status affords increased autonomy. Powerful employees are free to express a wider range of emotions, in part because they make, model, and enforce organizational norms. Informal communication rules typically prohibit low-power employees from directly expressing hostility at their leaders, and if anger happens to "slip out" they may feel compelled to apologize quickly. In contrast, supervisors may feel little compunction about expressing anger, believing it their prerogative to do so when workers need correcting or motivating. Going further, employees may even *expect* such displays, viewing them as a "normal" supervisory response to performance failures. When supervisors violate these emotional expectations in a positive manner, by remaining calm rather than "exploding," displaying sympathy rather than casting blame, employees may respond with feelings of surprise, relief, or even admiration. Thus, leaders can exploit their emotional autonomy in ways that have potent and potentially long-term effects on the quality of their relationships with lower-status workers.

The behavioral repertoire of lower-status members is comparatively constrained. Nonetheless, they often use emotional communication to negotiate, rather deftly, the contours of the leader–member relationship. For example, to be effective in their jobs, members must convince their leaders to provide scarce resources, accept new ideas, or grant exceptions to rules

113

(Waldron, 1994). The "upward influence tactics" that employees use for these purposes often involve the management of emotion (Waldron and Sanderson, 2011). Some leaders feel threatened by attempts to influence them, which they interpret as a usurpation of power or an effort to change the ground rules of the relationship. In response, members adopt tactics that assuage these feelings. For example, they might use flattery or ingratiation to boost feelings of liking and activate friendship obligations. The theory is that a friendly boss may feel more comfortable in granting favors. Another approach is to reduce a supervisor's fear of change by requesting a "trial period" in which a modest request is agreed to. Once the boss feels confident that deleterious consequences are unlikely, the employee makes a larger request. On occasion, low-status employees use guilt-based influence tactics, by implying that the supervisor "owes them" due to past sacrifices (i.e., a history of hard work; willingness to work overtime). Still rarer are fear-based tactics, in which employees threaten to circumvent the boss or quit (Kassing, 2007).

Abusers and bullies: Because low-status employees are vulnerable, leader–member relationships can be sites of abuse. Organizational researcher Benjamen Tepper (2000) has documented the nature of what he labels "abusive supervision." Among the hurtful behaviors Tepper observes is the sustained display of emotional hostility. To illustrate, he quotes these abusive lines uttered by an employer depicted in David Mamet's 1984 play *Glengarry Glen Ross*.

> What did I tell you the first day? Your thoughts are nothing; you are nothing . . . If you were in my toilet bowl I wouldn't bother flushing it. My bath mat means more to me than you . . . You don't like it here, leave!

Tepper argues that abusive supervision should be understood within an organization's system of justice. When indignant or humiliated employees perceive that the organization will take their grievance seriously, the effects of abuse may be muted. In another line of research, abusive supervision is considered a form of bullying, which among its many exploitative forms includes public humiliation or fear-inducing threats (Lutgen-Sandvik, Namie, and Namie, 2009). Lutgen-Sandvik and colleagues report that 30–37 percent of US workers have been bullied at some point in their careers. Bullying can be initiated by peers, but, as noted in chapter 5, it is often powerful people who use emotional communication in the interest of tyranny. Victims of bullying report a variety of negative effects, including decreased self-confidence at work, stress-related illness, and the desire to quit their jobs.

Sick supervisory relationships: Employees spend long hours on their jobs, sometimes under stressful conditions, so it is not surprising that relational pathologies sometimes crop up. Surviving sick relationships is the theme of a number of popular books, such as *Working for You isn't Working for Me: The Ultimate Guide to Managing Your Boss* (Crowley and Ester, 2009). In some cases, the dysfunction is an extension of relational proclivities that employees developed outside of work. For example, some supervisors enact outdated gender roles, expecting female employees to be subservient and males to be highly aggressive. Other employees become emotionally dependent on work. The emotional highs and ego support they receive from their co-workers cannot be matched in their personal relationships. The result is everlonger work hours and increasing disengagement from family and friends.

Leaders and members can develop an unhealthy emotional codependence. The spouse of a highly committed accountant (Shawn) described his relationship with a mercurial senior manager (Art). Their relationship mimics the cycle of emotional abuse that one finds in unhealthy domestic partnerships.

> They both are insanely committed to the company. For them, there is nothing quite like working for [company X]. But Art has no life. He works day and night. He literally lives and breathes his work and he expects Shawn to do that too. When something goes even a little bit wrong, Art screams and yells at everyone. He calls the employees names and berates them like they were naughty kids. Shawn is like the oldest son. He is held most responsible and gets yelled at all of the time. But Art also adores Shawn and he apologizes to him and

even gives him gifts and compliments after one of these episodes. Shawn always forgives Art for his bad behavior. Shawn says he "gets" Art. He thinks Art really wants to control his anger, but his love for [company X] just gets in the way.

Peer Relationships

Peer relationships are important sites of both positive and negative emotional communication. Indeed, the emotional tone of interactions with colleagues may be reflected in the degree of satisfaction that an employee finds in work and in life. Here I consider workplace friendships, creative partnerships, and team relationships.

Workplace friendships

It is not surprising that friendships form at work, given that employees spend much time together, inhabit common space, share organizational values, and are required to cooperate on tasks (Bridge and Baxter, 1992). Organizational communication researcher Patricia Sias has studied peer relationships extensively, finding that employees view them as sources of enjoyment, creativity, and advice (Sias, 2006). Most relevant to the current topic, Sias sees these social ties as important sources of emotional support. It is in relationships with friendly colleagues that workers share joys and vent frustrations. These interactions help workers interpret ambiguous emotional messages, make sense of their own ambivalent feelings, and recharge emotional resources (Waldron and Kassing, 2011: chapter 3). Healthy peer relationships certainly help employees weather difficult moments, but they do more than ward off emotional threats. They are central to a meaningful and vibrant working life (Dutton and Heaphy, 2003).

Emotionally difficult relationships

Unfortunately, peers can also be potent sources of emotional distress. Sias and her colleagues studied the causes of friendship deterioration as reported by a diverse sample of employees (Sias, Heath, Perry, Silva, and Fix, 2004). Several of them related to emotional communication. One reported cause, *problem person-alities,* involved annoying personality traits, including a proclivity for self-pity or excessive emotional sensitivity. Based on my own work on the relational dimensions of emotion, this kind of peer is hyper-vigilant for potential slights, easily offended, and frequently found to be in an "emotional huff" (Waldron, 2000).

Sias and colleagues (2004) identified *promotion* and *betrayal* as additional causes of friendship decay. The promotion of a friend occasionally resulted in problematic feelings of envy. Perceived betrayal is another potent source of workplace emotion (Waldron and Krone, 1991), particularly when presumed friends reveal con-fidences, engage in "back-stabbing," or take unfair credit for one's own work. These events lead to expressions of hurt and anger, and they may poison the larger social network to which the parties belong, to include common friends, family members, and leaders (Waldron, 2003). In response to these various forms of relation-ship deterioration, peers may choose to terminate the relationship. Sias and Perry (2004) studied these termination strategies, some of which involved emotional communication. The *depersonalization* approach curtailed informal communication with the peer, which presumably included the disclosure of private feelings. The *cost escalation* approach included the elicitation of negative emotions in the former friend through such tactics as condescension and criticism.

Other kinds of peer relationships can turn problematic. In maintaining mixed-sex relationships, workers may be particularly careful to regulate emotions to prevent peers from "getting the wrong impression." A study of the relationship maintenance tactics used by female workers suggested that, compared to males, they report being more proactive in managing emotional displays and avoiding appearances of emotional intimacy (Waldron, Foreman, and Miller, 1993). This finding is further evidence that cultural biases, including gendered ones, influence emotional labor. In most cultures, women are more likely to find their emotional behavior evaluated and "sexualized" and they are more often victims of sexual harassment. For those reasons, female employees may be more conscious of, and controlled in, their emotional displays.

Another example of emotionally difficult communication arises when feelings of affection between colleagues turn to love (Quinn, 1977). Workplace romances are obviously fulfilling for the participants and some of these blossom to be long-term partnerships. Some organizations encourage workplace romance but most try to regulate it in some way (Belkin, 2004). One reason for caution is that failed romance sometimes leads to charges of sexual harassment (Pierce and Aguinis, 2001). The intensity of romantic connections can complicate relations with co-workers, who may be (for example) cautious about sharing confidential information with one partner for fear that the message will be shared with the other. Perceptions of favoritism are another source of bad feeling. Later, if the romance fails, the former lovers (and their co-workers) may have a difficult time negotiating feelings of hurt or hostility.

Peer relationships can be sources of other unpleasant emotions, such as jealousy or guilt. Jealousy arises when one's relationship with a peer is threatened by co-workers who make claims on his or her time or attention. Employees feel guilty when they violate the informal rules that govern peer relations. It is an emotion that can be easily manipulated by peers (or supervisors).

Kayla, a software developer for a hard-driving start-up company "turned off her guilt meter" after she recognized that it was unnecessary to emulate the work habits of her overzealous co-workers, who toiled at the office nearly every night and weekend, but also complained about a string of failed relationships. By striking a reasonable balance between her obligations to co-workers and family members, Kayla released herself from the grip of unreasonable relational expectations.

Team relationships

Work is increasingly organized around teams, but teamwork has both "bright" and "dark" sides (for thorough reviews, see

Seibold, Kang, Gailliard, and Jahn, 2009; Thompson and Hoon-Seok, 2006). When compared to individual efforts, work in teams can be more emotionally rewarding and more frustrating. In teams, members often collaborate to create emotional experiences. For example, to encourage a dispirited member, they might engage in a round of esteem-boosting compliments. More negatively, the team might hold an informal complaint session in order to shame those members who have failed to meet task deadlines. Members will occasionally "gang up" on poor performers, scaring them with threats and extracting expressions of remorse. The emotional impact of messages communicated by peers may account for the popularity of "360 degree feedback" programs in which workers receive performance feedback from status-equal teammates as well as leaders (Atwater and Waldman, 1998). This approach capitalizes on the well-known effects of peer pressure, which for our purposes can be conceptualized as collective efforts to intensify the emotional bonds that motivate performance.

Creative partnerships

Teams are often expected to be creative, but the collective activity that spawns creativity can be found in other relational contexts. A field study of creative organizations, including the one that developed the wildly successful "pump" shoe, revealed the central role of a diverse and loosely connected network of creative people and technical experts (Hargadon and Bechky, 2006). These sometimes involved temporary and fleeting forms of contact, including brainstorming sessions, unscheduled consultations in hallways, aggressive question-and-answer sequences, and the sharing of creativity-inducing metaphors. The principals in these "creative collectives" were united by a variety of communication practices, some of which were emotional. For example, they rarely expressed fear of ridicule, even when ideas seemed implausible. Experts were willing to put aside their scheduled tasks to help colleagues who needed creative assistance. In other words, they rarely expressed the kinds of exasperation or scorn that can squelch creative

119

thinking. Unhindered by envy or jealousy, members freely shared their ideas and shared the credit. Those who championed new ideas entertained thought-provoking suggestions and probing questions without having their feelings hurt. They were emotionally thick-skinned during these interactions even as they received an emotional charge from the creative process.

Relational Functions of Emotional Communication

Although work relationships take a variety of forms, the functions of emotional communication are relatively similar across relational types. I describe some of them below.

Provoking

One possible evolutionary function of emotional communication is to negotiate power relations through provocation. This is often accomplished through the communicative act of teasing (see Keltner, 2009). Gentle teasing typically elicits embarrassment, but it can also yield feelings of solidarity and belonging when the tone of the teaser is friendly and care is taken to avoid serious threat to the "victim's" face. However, teasing can be used to provoke a reaction in targets. If they react with expressions of hostility, the teaser knows to "back off." Phrases such as "Just teasing!" allow the teaser to deny harmful intent and, perhaps, escape retaliation. From an evolutionary perspective, these kinds of emotional exchanges allow members of an organization to negotiate boundaries without engaging in more direct and damaging conflict.

Detecting/anticipating

Some co-workers have an uncanny ability to detect the feelings of co-workers and anticipate the relational consequences. They are the first ones to know when a colleague is upset by a family matter. In meetings, they pay close attention to the non-verbal cues that signal frustration, impatience, or embarrassment. This sensitivity to emotional messages, a kind of *emotional radar*, can be advantageous in work teams. Emotional radar leads to early detection of group tensions. With a humorous quip, a process-oriented suggestion ("Let's go back to that concern that Rita expressed earlier") or a face-supporting compliment, these emotional specialists can change the tone of a meeting and resuscitate team morale. As noted in chapter 1, the capacity to detect emotion is a valued aspect of communication competence, especially when other employees are emotionally impervious. It is one of the intangibles that help employees navigate the social terrain of the organization, one of the factors that make an employee "good with people."

Maintaining

Although emotional episodes are often implicated in relationship decline, the communication of feeling is also central in the maintenance of relationships. Relationship maintenance refers to processes that stabilize and preserve relationships, often through the ordinary and routine kinds of discourse that pervade daily life (Tepper, 1995; Waldron, 1991, 2003). In leader–member relationships, at least five relationship maintenance patterns have been identified.

- *Personal:* frequent small talk, discussion of personal plans and problems, and the use of humor are common. From the standpoint of emotion, willingness to disclose personal feelings is the defining feature.
- *Contractual:* this is a task-oriented approach with an emphasis on rule compliance and meeting of expectations. Emotional displays are limited to organizationally legitimized feelings, such as showing enthusiasm for organizational objectives and values.
- *Regulative:* the relationship is maintained by avoidance and not making a poor relationship worse. Conflict is strictly limited. Emotional displays are carefully edited.
- *Direct:* relational expectations are discussed explicitly and

perceived relational injustices are questioned. Emotion is expressed with little editing.

- *Extra-contractual*: exceeding expectations. Work relationships are prioritized over personal relationships. Personal feelings are discounted and employees engage in "deep acting," in which organizationally mandated feelings are experienced as one's own.

Workers may pay little conscious attention as they enact these patterns of communication, but relationship maintenance efforts lay the emotional groundwork upon which more taxing episodes are played out. For example, those who maintain their relationship by carefully avoiding emotional encounters (regulative tactics) may be caught off-guard when conflict situations become emotional. Unpracticed in the art of expressing their feelings in constructive ways, these employees may also be cowed by emotive colleagues. In contrast, those who disclose personal feelings routinely (personal tactics) or baldly (direct tactics) may find emotive conflict to be "normal" or even refreshing in its bluntness.

Tipping

The repetitive nature of organizational interactions causes low-level emotional responses to build, deepen, and intensify until they reach a relational tipping point. Interestingly, it is often these intense feelings, rather than the mild ones, that sometimes get expressed. Consider this report from "Roger," a faculty member whose initial irritation built over the course of several days until he inappropriately unloaded on a colleague.

I was trying to schedule a meeting with three other people to discuss the case of a student who had admitted to cheating. We were all on the committee that reviewed these matters. On Monday, I sent out an email asking for available days/times. At first, only one member responded that she was free on Friday afternoon. I was kind of annoyed that the others didn't respond by Tuesday afternoon, so I sent another email. No response. So I called them both and left voice mails and I guess my tone of voice indicated my growing impatience. One of these faculty members emailed back, telling me Friday was OK for the meeting, but added in all-capital letters to "COOL YOUR JETS." Of course, he copied all four of us on the message! Now I was feeling quite irritated and a little humiliated. So when the third member called back on Thursday to remind me that she was out of town at a conference and could not attend on Friday, I just snapped: "Fine! You plan the frigging meeting!" It was total overreaction on my part and I later apologized, but my emotion just reached a tipping point.

Intensifying

The disclosure of otherwise "private emotions" may signal affection, even intimacy, in work relationships. By sharing such feelings as envy for a co-worker, deep frustration with the job, or the joy of a successful project, workers come to know one another more deeply. These kinds of communication are not required by the work role and they suggest a developing sense of trust. Emotional sharing may in itself produce more intense emotional bonds. Indeed, it is not uncommon for co-workers to fall in love, although organizations vary in the extent to which they prohibit or regulate this particular emotion. For a thorough review of recent research on organizational romance, see Waldron and Kassing (2011: chapter 6). Of course, the putting aside of emotional regulations may indicate a less positive form of intensification, as indicated by comments of the type, "To be perfectly honest, I hate your guts." Expressions of hostility in an otherwise cordial work environment are akin to declarations of war – the usual rules of constraint no longer apply.

Forgiving

The communication of forgiveness has received considerable attention in the literature on personal relationships (Waldron and Kelley, 2008). But researchers are increasingly considering its relevance in the workplace (Metts, Cupach, and Lippert, 2006).

Waldron and Kelley defined forgiveness as a process of relational communication:

> Forgiveness is a relational process whereby harmful conduct is acknowledged by one or both partners; the harmed partner extends undeserved mercy to the perceived transgressor; one or both partners experience a transformation from negative to positive states, and the meaning of the relationship is renegotiated, with the possibility of reconciliation. (Waldron and Kelley, 2008: 5)

According to them, emotional communication is crucial in the forgiveness process. Emotional reactions are inevitable after serious transgressions. Forgiveness rarely proceeds until emotions are acknowledged and legitimized by both parties. In addition, the expression of remorse is typically a signal that transgressors understand the harm they have created and are willing to make amends. As mentioned above, relational harm is not unusual in organizations. Organizations that create processes for workers to pursue forgiveness may increase the likelihood that frayed relational bonds can be repaired.

Soothing

A key function of emotional communication in work relationships is soothing those who are agitated, troubled, or upset. This form of communication happens frequently in interactions with customers, who may be unhappy about the quality of a service or product. Customer-service clerks calm customers by acknowledging the legitimacy of their emotions, apologizing for their inconvenience, and (often) pledging to remove or repair the circumstances that are feeding the emotion. Leaders sometimes soothe the fears of members who are disconcerted by organizational change. In another example, peers may feel compelled to offer consolation when a colleague fails to receive a promotion or suffers a personal setback. Soothing is enacted through the comforting behaviors discussed in chapter 1, but as an emotional communication practice, it may have lasting relational implications. Soothing is a humane act of kindness that may strengthen or confirm relational ties between organization members, beyond what might be expected if work were strictly results- and task-oriented And, as a practical matter, soothing may convince upset employees not to vent their disappointment in ways that are destructive to their relationships and careers.

Remembering/reconstructing

Co-workers share histories, sometimes long ones, and the reconstructing of the past produces and reproduces important relational feelings. The recollection of past triumphs generates feelings of pride and bolsters hope for future achievements. Peers may ruefully recall past mistakes – times when feelings were hurt by rash comments or misunderstandings. The resulting feelings of humility counter any tendencies toward hubris and encourage more careful relational behavior in the present. The sharing of humorous anecdotes from the past serves to relieve anxiety, build affection, and make work fun.

Developing/maturing

Communication is one way that workers develop emotional maturity in their ranks. Often they do so by helping each other develop the emotional hardiness that is called for in current work circumstances. "It's time to put on your big-girl panties," "buck up," and "you have to be thick-skinned," are just three colloquial phrasings of this familiar sentiment. At other times, the emotional message conveys a sense that expectations have not been met. When a supervisor expresses "disappointment" in one of her employees, she is suggesting that her own emotions are a barometer of the employee's development. The disappointment is often offered with a tone of relational concern, suggesting that the supervisor really cares about the employee, but expected a better performance. This kind of emotional communication can be parental in tone, as if more experienced employees see it as their duty to challenge and prepare their less emotionally savvy peers.

Conclusion

Organizational relationships come in a bewildering variety of forms, but they are all sustained by emotional communication. Due to space limitations some of these received little attention in this chapter. For example, mentoring relationships can be crucial sources of emotional support. The emotional regulations that govern formal leader–member relationships may be relaxed when protégés communicate with mentors. Several emotionally potent relationships were not covered here, because they are addressed in other chapters. In chapter 3 ("Emotional Occupations"), the relationship between coaches and athletes is examined. So too are the emotional connections that develop between spiritual leaders and their followers. Chapter 5 examines in more detail the abusive practices of emotional tyrants – powerful people who use communication to manipulate the feelings of others.

Almost since its inception, scholars in the field of communication have emphasized that nearly every message conveys relational meanings in addition to other information. In organizations these relational messages concern power, trust, and belonging. Emotion is complexly tied up in this relationship-sustaining role of communication. It is sometimes a reaction to communication that affirms or violates relationships with co-workers. And, just as important, by disclosing feelings co-workers intensify their bonds, maintain them, and sometimes terminate them. Emotional communication can be an instrument of relational manipulation, but it also vitalizes the complex network of human connections that forms the core of any organization.

References

Atwater, L. E., and Waldman, D. A. (1998). Introduction: 360-degree feedback and leadership development. *Leadership Quarterly*, 9: 423–6.

Bass, B. M., and Riggio, R. E. (2006). *Transformationl Leadership* (2nd edn). Mahwah, NJ: Lawrence Erlbaum Publishers.

Belkin, L. (2004). St. Valentine, he's in human resources. *New York Times* (February 15), p. 10/1.

Bridge, K., and Baxter, L. A. (1992). Blended relationships: friends as work associates. *Western Journal of Communication*, 56: 200–25.

Buzzanell, P. M., Shenoy, S., Remke, R. V., and Lucas, K. (2009). Responses to destructive organizational contexts: intersubjectively creating resilience to foster human dignity and hope. In P. Lutgen-Sandvick and B. Davenport-Sypher (eds), *Destructive Organizational Communication: Processes, Consequences, and Constructive Ways of Organizing*. New York: Routledge, pp. 293–315.

Carsten, M. K., Uhl-Bien, M., West, B.J., Patera, J. L., and McGregor, R. (2010). Exploring social constructions of followership: a qualitative study. *The Leadership Quarterly*, 21: 543–62.

Collinson, D. (2006). Rethinking followership: a post-structuralist analysis of follower identities. *Leadership Quarterly*, 17: 179–89.

Conger, J. (1999). Charismatic and transformational leadership in organizations: an Insider's perspective on these developing streams of research. *The Leadership Quarterly*, 10: 145–79.

Crowley. K., and Ester, K. (2009). *Working for You isn't Working for Me: The Ultimate Guide to Managing Your Boss*. New York: Portfolio/Penguin Group.

Dutton, J. E., and Heaphy, E. (2003). Coming to life: the power of high quality connections at work. In K. Cameron., J. Dutton, and R. Quinn (eds), *Positive Organizational Scholarship*. San Francisco, CA: Barrett Koehler, pp. 779–814.

Fisher, A. (2010). Help! My boss keeps putting me down (January 13). Accessed at: <http://money.cnn.com/2010/01/13/news/economy/bad_bosses.fortune/index.htm>.

Gardner, W. L., Avolio, B. J., Luthans, F., May, D. R., and Walumbwa, F. O. (2005). "Can you see the real me?": a self-based model of authentic leader and follower development. *The Leadership Quarterly*, 16: 343–72.

George, B. (2003). *Authentic Leadership: Rediscovering the Secrets to Creating Lasting Value*. San Francisco, CA: Jossey-Bass.

Graham, J. W. (1991). Servant-leadership in organizations: inspirational and moral. *The Leadership Quarterly*, 2: 105–19.

Graham, J. W. (1995). Leadership, moral development, and citizenship behavior. *Business Ethics Quarterly*, 5: 43–54.

Haidt, J. (2003). The moral emotions. In R. J. Davidson, K. R. Scherer, and H. H. Goldsmith (eds), *Handbook of Affective Sciences*. Oxford: Oxford University Press, pp. 852–70.

Hargadon, A. B., and Bechky, B. A. (2006). When collections of creatives become creative collectives: a field study of problem solving at work. *Organization Science*, 17: 484–504.

Kassing, J. W. (2006). Employees' expressions of upward dissent as a function of current and past work experiences. *Communication Reports*, 19: 79–88.

Kassing, J. W. (2007). Going around the boss: exploring the consequences of circumvention. *Management Communication Quarterly*, 21: 55–74.

Keltner, D. (2009). *Born To Be Good: The Science of a Meaningful Life*. New York: W. W. Norton & Company.

Larson, J. R. (1989). The dynamic interplay between employee's feedback-seeking strategies and supervisor's delivery of performance feedback. *Academy of Management Review*, 14: 408–22.

Lutgen-Sandvik, P., Namie, G., and Namie, R. (2009). Workplace bullying: causes, consequences, and corrections. In P. Lutgen-Sandvik and B. Sypher (eds), *Destructive Organizational Communication*. New York: Routledge, pp. 27–52.

Metts, S., Cupach, W. R., and Lippert, L. (2006). Forgiveness in the workplace. In. J. M. Harden-Fritz and B. L. Ohmdahl (eds), *Problematic Relationships in the Workplace*. N ew York: Peter Lang Publishing, pp. 249–78.

Northhouse, P. G. (2010). *Leadership: Theory and Practice* (5th edn). Thousand Oaks, CA: Sage.

Pierce, C. A., and Aguinis, H. (2001). A framework for investigating the link between Workplace romance and sexual harassment. *Group and Organization Management*, 26: 206–29.

Quinn, R. (1977). Coping with cupid: the formation, impact, and management of romantic relationships in organizations. *Administrative Science Quarterly*, 22: 30–45.

Rosen, S., and Tesser, A. (1970). On reluctance to communicate undesirable information: the MUM effect. *Sociometry*, 33: 253–63.

Seibold, D. R., Kang, P., Gailliard, B. M., and Jahn, J. (2009). Communication that damages teamwork: the dark side of teams. In P. Lutgen-Sandvik and B. Davenport-Sypher (eds), *Destructive Organizational Communication: Processes, Consequences, and Constructive Ways of Organizing*. New York: Routledge, pp. 267–89.

Sias, P. M. (2006). Workplace friendship deterioration. In. J. M. Harden-Fritz and B. L. Ohmdahl (eds), *Problematic Relationships in the Workplace*. New York: Peter Lang, pp. 69–88.

Sias, P. M., and Perry, T. (2004). Disengaging from work relationships: a research note. *Human Communication Research*, 30: 589–602.

Sias, P. M., Heath, R. G., Perry, T., Silva, D., and Fix, B. (2004). Narratives of workplace friendship deterioration. *Journal of Social and Personal Relationships*, 21: 321–40.

Tepper, B. (1995). Upward maintenance tactics in supervisory mentoring and nonmentoring relationships. *Academy of Management Journal*, 38: 1191–1205.

Tepper, B. (2000). Consequences of abusive supervision. *Academy of Management Journal*, 42: 100–8.

Thompson, L. L., and Hoon-Seok, C. (2006). *Creativity and Innovation in Organizational Teams*. New York: Routledge.

Tracey, S. (2009). Managing burnout and moving toward employee engagement: Reinvigorating the study of stress at work. In P. Lutgen-Sandvik and B. Davenport-Sypher (eds), *Destructive Organizational Communication: Processes, Consequences, and Constructive Ways of Organizing*. New York: Routledge, pp. 9–26.

Wagoner, R., and Waldron, V. R. (1999). How supervisors convey routine bad news: facework at UPS. *The Southern Communication Journal*, 64: 193–210.

Waldron, V. (1991). Achieving communication goals in superior–subordinate relationships: the multi-functionality of upward maintenance tactics. *Communication Monographs*, 58: 289–306.

Waldron, V. (1994). Once more, *with feeling*. Reconsidering the role of emotion in work. In S. Deitz (ed.), *Communication Yearbook 17*. New York: Lawrence Erlbaum Publishers, pp. 388–416.

Waldron, V. (2000). Relational experiences and emotion at work. In S. Fineman (ed.), *Emotion in Organizations* (2nd edn). London: Sage, pp. 64–82.

Waldron, V. (2003). Relationship maintenance in organizational settings. In D. J. Canary and M. Dainton (eds), *Maintaining Relationships through Communication: Relational, Contextual, and Cultural Variations*. Mahwah, NJ: Lawrence Erlbaum, pp. 163–84.

Waldron V. (2009). Emotional tyranny at work: suppressing the moral emotions. In P. Lutgen-Sandvik and B. Davenport-Sypher (eds). *Destructive Organizational Practices: Processes, Consequences, and Constructive Ways of Organizing*. New York: Routledge, pp. 9–26.

Waldron, V., and Kassing, J. (2011). *Managing Risk in Communication Encounters: Strategies for the Workplace*. Los Angeles, CA: Sage.

Waldron, V., and Kelley, D. (2008). *Communicating Forgiveness*. Los Angeles, CA: Sage Publications.

Waldron, V., and Krone, K. J. (1991). The experience and expression of emotion in the workplace: a study of a corrections organization. *Management Communication Quarterly*, 4: 287–309.

Waldron, V. R., and Anderson, J. (2011). The role of subjective threat in upward influence situations. *Communication Quarterly*, 59: 239–54.

Waldron, V., Foreman, C., and Miller, R. (1993). Managing gender conflicts in the supervisory relationship: relationship definition strategies used by women and men. In G. Kreps (ed.), *Sexual Harassment: Communication Implications*. Cresskill, NJ: Hammond Press, pp. 234–56.

5

Emotion and Organizational Morality

I was flabbergasted by the way the new management team was treating people in my old department. These people had been loyal to the organization and to me. Now they were being exploited or just ignored. The new boss insisted that they move across town to be closer to his office, but he never asked them about it. It didn't matter anyway because he never answered their questions or returned their calls. Most of his decisions were communicated through snippy text messages. One time he even ended a major project with a text, with no other explanation! It's just wrong to treat good people that way! The unit is tanking now, with people working ridiculous amounts of hours with almost no resources and no support from the guy who should be their boss. It is shameful and it makes me angry enough to actually speak up about it, even though I really have no right to jump in at this point. Needless to say, my former co-workers feel a lot of resentment and they are looking for new jobs. It is sad, because it doesn't need to be this way. Just treat people with some respect and they usually will work their butts off for the company!

This experience was shared by Rob, a former project manager who was recently promoted to a leadership position in another department. As the story unfolds, it becomes increasingly emotional. Rob describes the new boss's behavior as shameful, his own response as angry, the co-workers as resentful, and the situation as sad. His use of exclamation points provides emotional urgency to the tale. As is the case with so many of the emotional narratives I have collected over the years, these feelings are linked to what

Rob sees as a moral infraction. His language frames the issue not so much as one of managerial incompetence or lost productivity, but as a matter of right and wrong. Rob is sharing his sense of how leadership practices are varying from what "should" or "ought to" be. The new boss, with his detached style and insensitive text messages is "wrong" for failing to respect "good" people. Rob seems to be morally outraged and his co-workers are resentful toward what appears to be unjust treatment. He has no "right" to involve himself, but Rob's anger is compelling him to "speak up."

Chapter 5 examines the role of emotional discourses in expressing and shaping the moral codes that govern organizations and their members. First, I examine the "signal" function of emotion – its capacity to make individuals and organizations aware of the potential for harm or wrongdoing. Second, drawing from a long tradition of philosophical and social-scientific thought, I explore the "moral emotions" and how they are expressed at work. Examples include indignation, pride, and remorse. The interesting case of shame is considered, as are collective practices of shaming, mobbing, public embarrassment, and "cooling out" aggrieved co-workers. A third focus of this chapter is the concept of *emotional tyranny*, the efforts of the powerful to use emotion in ways that are harmful to others. Drawing from previous work (Waldron, 2009), I argue that these abusive practices undermine the signal function of emotion, making it more difficult for employees to detect, interpret, and report violations of the organization's moral code. Chapter 5 also examines the role of emotion in discriminatory work practices, with a particular focus on sexual harassment and gender discrimination.

The Signal Function of Emotion

Emotional experiences mark meaningful and important episodes in working lives that can otherwise be dulled by highly predictable routines, bureaucratic regulation, and mundane interactions. Experiences become emotional because they *matter* to us. Emotional counters are sometimes novel and "worth talking about" as we share the content of our work days with friends or family members. The emotion is a signal that we need to "make meaning" from experiences by thinking and talking about them. Feelings of intense pride may be a sign that our work identity has been supported by leaders. In contrast, "hurt" feelings may be in reaction to identity threats, as when a co-worker questions one's commitment or integrity. Emotions are often reactions to violations of expectation, positive or negative, but we may need to consult with others to become fully aware of what those expectations are. Emotions signal danger. They may prompt employees to consider the possibility that a relationship will be a source of trouble, an organization is at risk, or a career is in jeopardy. Organizations that tend to the emotional climate of the workplace are more likely to detect lapses in ethical conduct and recognize unfairness in the treatment of employees. All of these examples illustrate what researchers have called the "signal function" of emotion.

Signaling danger

Among the earliest views of emotions are those that conceptualize it as a survival mechanism (Darwin, 1872; James, 1884). This perspective and its later variations view emotions such as fear as one step in a sequence of responses (recreated below) to potentially dangerous environmental stimuli.

> 1. Encounter a bear → 2. Appraise as dangerous → 3. Physiological arousal →4. Run! → 5. Label the experience as "fear."

Over the years, debates have raged over the ordering of these steps (Lazarus, 1984; Zajonc, 1984). Do the physiological responses to the bear come first (the surge of adrenalin, running), or is it the cognitive appraisal ("Is this a dangerous animal? Should I fight or run?")? However, the central role of biologically based emotional reactions to danger is clear (for a recent review, see Keltner, 2009). Although few workers encounter bears in the course of their daily activities, many do face potentially hazardous working conditions, grumpy supervisors, angry customers, or unethical co-workers. Their feelings in these encounters shape the "fight-or-flight" response, as indicated in statements such as these:

> "I could sense that trouble was brewing, so I steered clear of that whole situation."

> "Anger boiled up in me and I just told the customer to 'back off'."

> "I just felt bad about the decision. My conscience was telling me to say something."

> "I could smell fear in the room. People were afraid they would be caught."

> "We all felt vaguely guilty. Could we really make money this way?"

In these cases, employees describe a kind of "emotional radar," a type of warning system. It prompts employees to circumvent dangerous conditions (flight) or defend themselves more aggressively (fight).

Signaling moral jeopardy and moral decay

Although workplace danger comes in many forms, including physical harm and career damage, it often has moral implications. Feelings of anxiety or guilt may be signs that personal or organizational moral codes are threatened (Freud, 1961; Hochschild, 1983). The "smell of fear" may be a collective emotional response, a palpable indication that a group will soon be held accountable for conspiring to violate moral standards. A lack of remorse may indicate that a person or organization lacks a moral conscience. "How do you sleep at night?" might be the response of a client who is misled or treated unjustly by an organization. From these examples, it is clear that the signal function of emotion extends to its role as the moral conscience of individuals and workers.

Moral signaling has broad implications for an organization's reputation and its accountability to societal standards. At the time of this writing, two high-profile examples come to mind. First, the US economy is still reeling in the aftermath of the arguably immoral behavior of mortgage lenders and some of their customers. Faced with the very real risk of default, lenders traditionally required borrowers to make significant down payments when purchasing a home and to provide evidence that their income was sufficient to make future payments. However, in recent years mortgage brokers dramatically relaxed these safeguards, encouraging even unqualified people to take out large loans. The reason? Regulation changes allowed lenders to "package-up" these risky loans and pass them on to unsuspecting investors in the form of complicated "derivatives." This process removed fear from the lending process, as lenders themselves would be unaffected when unqualified borrowers defaulted (as they did in droves, bringing the financial system to its knees). Normally, fear would have signaled risk, and the desire to increase safety would have protected lenders, their customers, and the larger lending system.

The second example involves President Barack Obama's decision to terminate the command of Stanley McChrystal, a previously well-respected four-star general in charge of the US war effort in Afghanistan. An article published in *Rolling Stone* magazine described the behavior of the general and key members of his staff during an unscripted conversation with a reporter, which eventually turned to the topic of the president and his cabinet. Apparently unaware that their comments would reach the American public, the military leaders adopted a mocking tone of voice, gleefully shared insults, and repeatedly disparaged such dignitaries as the ambassador to Afghanistan and the vice president and former senator, Joe Biden. Upon reading the article, President Obama was reported to be "angry" and he abruptly recalled the general to Washington for a face-to-face conversation. President Obama explained on national television that McChrystal's behavior violated the standards of conduct required of all soldiers, regardless of rank; undermined the working relationships of US leaders; and lacked the emotional maturity the nation expected of leaders during times of war. In short, the emotions displayed by the general and his staff were signals of moral decay and a lack of respect for the American tradition of civilian leadership of the armed forces.

Signaling face threat

As the sociologist Erving Goffman (1955) noted long ago, social coordination, including work, requires each actor to accept and acknowledge roles of various kinds. Doing so allows a routine transaction to proceed smoothly, with limited effort expended on negotiating roles and choosing appropriate behavior. Upon entering situations, actors behave in ways that signal their understanding of the social situation (e.g., this is a performance review, where one person offers evaluations and the other listens before responding). In doing so, they project a certain public version of the self, which Goffman called "face." An employee's face includes the qualities that he or she hopes others will accept (or at least not question in public), such as task competence, trustworthiness, or "coolness." Goffman argues that individuals are emotionally invested in their face. Indeed, emotional reactions of consternation, embarrassment, or humiliation signal that others have questioned, rejected, or simply ignored one's face. These are what Goffman calls "face-threatening" acts. Employees violate face without the assistance of others, by making very public mistakes or losing their composure.

If they notice displays of embarrassment, co-workers can sometimes swoop to the communicative rescue, by discounting the source of insults ("Don't listen to that jerk") or showing solidarity with the victim ("Listen, we all do embarrassing things in public. Don't worry about it"). This kind of face-sensitive communication is an expression of compassion, which in itself is a kind of moral commitment. These communicative moves to project, support, and threaten publicly presented selves are what Goffman (1955) called "facework." It becomes emotional when the social order and predictability that Goffman found to be so important, is intentionally or accidentally disrupted. In this way, emotions signal disruption of what "ought to" be and they prompt interactions to restore the order of things.

Moral Emotions at Work

Emotions have been associated with morality since ancient times, but the "moral emotions" have received renewed interest from scholars in recent years (Haidt, 2003; Planalp, 1999; Solomon, 1989). One of these is motivational psychologist Bernard Weiner (2006), who creates a prominent place for these emotions in his model of how people are motivated to respond (or not) to injustice. Organizational researchers have also documented the close association between employee emotions and their perceptions of injustice (Bies, 1987; Harlos and Pinder, 2000). Importantly, it is not just the emotions, but how employees talk about them, that has moral significance. A recent study of discourse about emotion concluded that its function may be "judicial, establishing and policing a repertoire of acceptable emotional behaviours" (Coupland et al., 2008: 339). Emotional expressions are regulated by cultural understandings of right and wrong feelings and they simultaneously function to enforce those social codes (see Armon-Jones, 1986; Waldron, 1994). In the US, we see this in such morally tinged expressions as "That is nothing to be proud of," "You should be sorry for what you did," and "I should feel guilty about this, but I really don't."

Weiner (2006), the psychologist, and scholars of the "social constructivist" school of emotion (Averhill, 1983) conceptualize anger and related feelings primarily as reactions to moral transgressions. "Anger is an accusation or a value judgment following from the belief that another 'could and should' have done otherwise" (p. 35). For example, members of a team are obligated to attend meetings and arrive at work on time. Over and above the rules imposed by an employer, most workers consider it the right thing to do. It is a moral obligation to those co-workers who depend on you. A consistent failure to arrive at work on time could prompt workers to question the moral character of the team member. Their feelings may progress from consternation, to resentment, to *anger*. Anger energizes the team members and motivates them to restore the moral order. Anger is a moral justification for action ("We were *so* angry that we just had to do something").

What might they do? They may attempt to: (1) educate the tardy member about moral obligations of teamwork; (2) make him or her feel guilty about the extra work she is creating for them; (3) act collectively to shame, a kind of "peer pressure"; (4) issue fear-provoking threats; or (5) request intervention from management. Note that these actions are motivated by the emotion of anger, and some of them use emotion to convey the moral lesson.

Weiner's motivational model suggests that an alternative response to the tardy team-member worker could be sympathy, another moral emotion. This feeling arises when ethically questionable behavior is attributable to uncontrollable external circumstances. In this instance, the worker may be hampered by the burdens of caretaking for a chronically ill parent, or by an unreliable daycare provider. In contrast to anger, sympathy could motivate workers to redress injustice by altering the co-worker's environment rather than his or her character. They may offer suggestions for caregiving help, ask the supervisor for assistance from temporary staff, or decide to simply shoulder more of the work themselves until the situation is resolved.

The case of the team member who arrives late to work illustrates that emotions are tied to employees' assessments of the moral requirements of work situations and their interpretations of efforts by the self, peers, and the larger organization to satisfy those requirements.

Documenting the moral emotions

My own studies of narratives reported by employees have yielded an extended list of moral emotions or, at least, feelings that employees link to moral concerns. Table 5.1 presents a typology of these emotions and the social circumstances that give rise to them. Of course, many of these can also be experienced in situations that have no obvious moral implications. People can be angry at traffic jams and they may be fearful because a large bear has arrived on the scene. Nonetheless, the emotions employees report feeling in their workplace interactions are often discussed in moral terms. For example, hope is an emotion associated with the promise of

Table 5.1 Some moral emotions and social referents*

Emotion	Social referents
Admiration	Success of deserving others
Bitterness	Sustained feelings of hostility toward unfair treatment; holding a grudge
Chagrin	A sense of vexation, indignity, or loss of face
Compassion	Caring, empathy in reference to the circumstances of other people
Delight	The moral character or practices of others exceeds expectations
Disappointment	Distress at the failures of esteemed persons; expectancy violations
Disgust	Feeling contaminated or revolted by immoral behavior
Embarrassment	Acts which reveal moral failures or create an appearance of moral failure
Envy	Desire for the qualities, possessions, or accolades possessed by others
Fulfillment	Completion of moral duties; satisfaction with self
Guilt	Responsibility for wrongdoing
Hope	The sense that justice will prevail in the long run
Humiliation	Threats to dignity; dehumanizing behaviors
Humility	Exposure to transcendent moral forces
Hurt	Social wounds inflicted unjustly by others
Indignation	Ire at the unfairness of a social situation or system
Jealousy	One's rightful role in a relationship is threatened by rivals
Outrage/anger	Fury aroused by the offensive acts of others
Pride	Personal or group accomplishments; recognition by valued others
Regret/remorse	Sorrow for having hurt others or made a serious mistake
Resentment	Sustained or acute ill-treatment by others
Scorn	Someone or something held in contempt
Schafenfreude	Shame experienced by another brings joy to the self
Shame	Disgraceful, unworthy, or dishonorable behavior
Shock/surprise	Unexpected moral violations or affirmations by others
Suffering	Feelings of pain in response to transgressions of self or others
Sweet revenge	Satisfaction from "settling the score"; retribution
Sympathy	Pain or distress of another brings feelings of pity
Trepidation	Fear of the consequences of moral infractions; misgivings

Note: For a shorter list, see Waldron, 2009: 15.

an improved future. It need not concern improvements in morality. After all, one can feel hopeful about a co-worker's recovery
from illness or improvements in the performance of the stock
market. But employees often reference the feeling of hope as they
project the moral trajectory of their working lives. One secretary
anticipated that fairness will prevail in the future: "I can only hope
that next year's [performance] review recognizes what I really
contribute around here." A colleague once observed, "You hope
that when these nasty administrators get promoted that someone
will recognize their true colors and send them packing." In other
words, justice may prevail in the future, even if it hasn't in the past.

In the case of hope, emotional communication is future directed.
It helps employees look past current wrongful conditions in anticipation of a righteous future. This capacity for *time-shifting* is one
means of categorizing the moral emotions. As another example,
consider expressions of regret or remorse. The spokesperson
who invokes these emotions in discussing the transgressions of
an organization is in essence trying to put them in the past. The
audience is asked to believe that the moral character of the organization is different now. A certain amount of suffering is expected
in these situations ("Our employees feel the pain of those families
that were hurt by these mistakes"), and may convince the public
that the organization really "gets" what it did wrong, and is now
"deserving" of forgiveness. Forgiveness for past bad behavior
is predicated on the belief that immoral behavior will not be
repeated in the future.

Another means of categorizing the moral emotions involves
audience presence. The presence of co-workers makes moral
codes more salient, intensifies emotional reactions, and assures
that the emotional experience is collective, not just individual.
In recognition of this principle, workers are often rewarded in
public ceremonies for demonstrating what the organizations
consider to be virtues of "good" employees – dedication to task,
safety-mindedness, trustworthiness, commitment to customer
satisfaction.

The presence of the audience intensifies the mostly pleasant
emotions experienced by the employee (pride, satisfaction), and

that amplification process continues for days as colleagues offer kind words, handshakes, and pats on the back. The public nature of the event creates opportunities for the audience to experience the emotion vicariously or to at least *anticipate* how it might feel if they, too, were truly good. The moral emotion of admiration is likely to spread across the workgroup and it may flare again as pictures of the ceremony appear in the company newsletter and the employee's name appears on the honorary plaque in the lobby.

The presence of an audience is crucial to the experience of other less pleasant feelings. Embarrassment, whether intentionally elicited by the comments of a co-worker or spontaneously arising from a social blunder, is one example (for more on intentional embarrassment, see Sharkey, 1997). Employees feel embarrassed when others notice that their behavior is badly out of synch with social or organizational norms, or inconsistent with the employee's face (Goffman, 1955). While it is possible to feel embarrassed in private (the audience in this case is imagined), the experience is amplified when an audience is physically present. Their reactions (raised eyebrows, guffaws) indicate that expectations have been violated and their subsequent behaviors (mocking, jeering, sympathetic looks, good-humored joking) deepen the embarrassment, diffuse it quickly, or transform it into another feeling, such as chagrin, rueful amusement, or anger.

High-status audiences can intensify feelings of embarrassment to something closer to mortification and fear. One store manager described this scenario:

> One morning I was in my store getting ready to open. I was so engulfed in work that I lost track of time. The store opened at 10 a.m. and at about 10.15 the phone rang and it was my district manager. She asked me why my store wasn't open. In a panic I lied and said it was. But she knew it wasn't because she was at a pay phone across the hall from my store! I was mortified and she was extremely upset.

Intentional embarrassment can be used gently to tease a co-worker, a move which can build feelings of camaraderie and acceptance, but it is also used more aggressively to make rivals look foolish or to put a smug supervisor in his or her "place." This last example speaks to the role of emotions in redressing status differences that seem unjustified. Audience presence is a key factor in an intense emotional practice designed to make others acutely aware of the ways in which they have violated the moral standards of the workplace community. Public humiliation or *shaming* is a collective form of emotional communication in which moral violators are put on display and subjected to public expressions of disapproval or disgust. The US Congress did this when it called major league baseball players to testify about their use of steroids and other banned substances. The players were reminded of the public's high expectations for athletes, scolded for failing to meet their obligations as well-paid role models of good sportsmanship, and condemned for flouting the rules of fair play. The intent of these ceremonies is to leave the violators feeling chastened while the larger community feel satisfied that its moral interests have been defended. Less dramatic examples happen in most workplaces, as when underperforming associates are "called out" in sales meetings, or the manager of a telemarketing operation posts in a public place the productivity scores of all employees.

Social locus is another criterion that can be useful in classifying moral emotions. The issue here is the social unit to which moral obligations apply. For example, the feeling of fulfillment refers to the moral accomplishments of the *self*, whereas admiration, delight, compassion, and sympathy are responses to the moral practices of *others*. It is of course possible to feel admiration or sympathy for the self, but communicating self-admiration puts one in danger of appearing boastful to co-workers and self-pity is rarely tolerated for long. The loci of emotions like guilt, jealousy, or disdain are largely relational, as they are responses to the obligations that govern close bonds. Organizations often cultivate relational "feelings" by encouraging social activities and the use of relational metaphors. I have heard workers describe their boss as a "mother to me," their co-workers as "family," and their conflicts as "sibling rivalry." Given these kinds of relational connections, we might expect employees to scorn those who abandon the family as they move to another job and to feel disdain for those who reveal "family secrets." It should not be surprising if members compete for the affections of organizational parent figures and feel jealousy toward those who achieve it. Jealousy is the feeling that one's "rightful" place in a valued relationship is threatened (Waldron, 2009).

Another locus for moral behavior is the larger organization. Workers who feel they have been treated unfairly by management, and citizens who feel "yanked around" by government bureaucracy, are likely to feel indignation. The sense that the whole system is corrupt, that moral decay is pervasive, leads to feelings of disgust.

Still other emotions are unique in the *moral force* with which they are associated. Waldron (2009) reported that workers sometimes describe *humility* as a positive reaction to astonishing acts of goodness or what they view as transcendent models of moral behavior. For example, a social worker reported that she was "humbled by the goodness" of colleagues who worked long hours at low pay to care for extremely ill AIDS patients. A national parks worker described being "awed" by such natural places as the Grand Canyon, which for him had the spiritual resonance of a holy place. Experiences of emotional *shock* or *outrage* often arise when taken-for-granted moral expectations are blatantly violated or powerfully exceeded. Co-workers are sometimes shocked when a hardworking colleague is unfairly reprimanded or laid off. They are stunned by a co-worker's "backstabbing" behavior and outraged by the barefaced lies of a political rival, or the transparent "brown-nosing" of those seeking favorable treatment from a supervisor.

Finally, some moral emotions can be understood as *expressions of justice*. An example was collected during a study of US factory workers located in the mid-South (Waldron et al., 1993), who reported that a newly promoted shop foreman embarrassed workers on the shop floor by mimicking their accents and taunting them. Convinced that their former co-worker had become insufferably full of himself, workers conspired to "humble" him through a series of practical jokes. In this way, workers experienced a satisfying sense of revenge for the morally repugnant treatment they had received. In the workplace, justice is often associated with equity and fairness. The allocation of rewards may delight workers who receive more than expected, even as it inspires disappointment or envy in those who believe they deserve better treatment. Over the long term, inequity fosters feeling of bitterness. Employees who have been treated inequitably may find some satisfaction when high performers "fall from grace," an emotion described by the German word *schadenfreude*. In extreme cases, under-benefited employees may seek to "settle the score" with those who treated them unfairly. They may do so through such morally repugnant acts as industrial sabotage or workplace violence, or by more constructive means such as obtaining a higher-paid job at a rival company. In the latter case, the resulting emotion might be described as "sweet revenge."

Moral Emotions and Communication Process

Thus far, I have discussed a variety of moral emotions. But what is the connection between communication and these emotions? Figure 1 depicts relationships between organizational morality, emotion, and communication as a cyclical process. It is adapted from my earlier work (Waldron, 2009: 17) and Weiner's (2006) discussion of the ways in which the moral emotions are linked to justice. As it turns out, communication plays an important role at several points in the cycle. As the figure suggests, the moral emotions are prompted by a presumed infraction of the societal or organizational codes of conduct that apply to the workplace. Let's assume that a supervisor is observed by office workers in the act of bullying a fellow employee. Although many immoral acts might be observed (e.g., "cooking the books," deceiving a customer), some are inherently communicative. In this case, the supervisor is observed to humiliate the employee by shouting in a loud and angry voice a series of derogatory labels at a "slacking co-worker." Step 2 involves an assessment of the act's morality and this too may include communicative action. For example, the victim may look beseechingly at his or her fellow workers, in search of their sympathy and moral support. The observers may

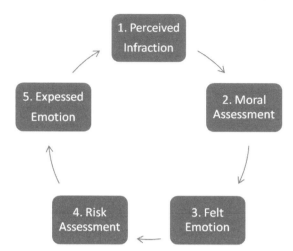

Figure 5.1 Communication of the moral emotions
*Destructive organisational communication: processes, consequences and constructive
ways of organizing* edited by Pam Lutgen-Sandvik. Copyright 2011

begin to whisper among themselves. *What is going on here? Is this
emotionally extravagant behavior justified in this situation? What
is the right and prudent thing to do when a colleague is subjected
to such apparently abusive treatment?* Having witnessed a morally
questionable emotional display, the audience may conclude that
the loud behavior *is* justified. Perhaps the offending employee
"had it coming" or in the past was unresponsive to calmer entreat-
ies. They may conclude that the supervisor "had no choice" but to
"lay down the law." In these cases, what originally appeared to be
unjustified bullying may be interpreted as a kind of rough justice.
In response, the audience may feel such moral emotions (Step 3)
as a collective sense of satisfaction or vindication, knowing that
justice is finally being served to an unproductive colleague. On the
other hand, the observers could attribute the loud behavior to a
well-known personality flaw of a supervisor who regularly "flies
off the handle" at the slightest provocation. Knowing that the
supervisor is abusing the privileges of the leader–member relationship, they may feel sympathy for their colleague, outrage at the

supervisor, and indignation toward the organization that allows such abuses to persist.

Will these feelings be expressed? That is the concern of Steps 4 and 5 in the cycle. First, the members make an assessment of risk (Step 4). They may wonder about the consequences of expressing outrage in this situation. How would it affect their relationships with the supervisor? The co-worker? Would expressing indignation to the human resource office result in a more just workplace, or would it create the likelihood of retaliation from a boss who is known to be a bully? Risk assessment could involve several rounds of interaction as employees and the victim contemplate their communicative options and consider the organization's moral track record as well as its procedures for redressing bad behavior. By remembering and reviewing the act the employees may trigger a new round of moral assessment ("This is abuse, not leadership"), emotion felt ("It makes me madder every time I think about it"), and risk assessment ("We can't afford to let this continue"). These actions may reverse, restart, and partially "replay" the cycle depicted in figure 5.1

In determining if and how to express moral emotions up the chain of command, the employees will consider a variety of tactics (also see Kassing, 2007). They may choose to reveal these feelings to the supervisor, remain silent, share the emotions only with family members or friends, or express their emotions to another powerful person. If choosing the latter, employees may hope to avoid creating the impression that they are "overreacting" by editing their message. For example, they could express "concern" rather than outrage. To make clear that the supervisor's emotional behavior violates broadly accepted codes of conduct (not just their personal preferences), employees might describe the behavior as a "shameful" breech of professional standards of which they remain "proud." To emphasize the ongoing nature of the abusive communication, they may describe themselves as indignant and long-suffering. Employees enact their acceptance or rejection of moral codes through these and other forms of discourse. In these ways, as depicted by the arrow connecting Step 5 back to Step 1, emotional communication is intricately bound up in a process of determining what counts as good and bad in our workplaces.

Emotional Tyranny

Recently, I have detailed the ways in which powerful (and not so powerful) people use emotional communication to manipulate and hurt others (Waldron, 2009). I call these practices "emotional tyranny." With reference to figure 5.1, emotional tyrants undermine the moral functioning of organizations at several points. For example, their emotional communication may itself constitute a kind of wrongdoing (as with the bullying supervisor above). However, these emotional manipulators may wreak moral havoc in other ways. For example, they may use emotion to convince workers that normal codes of conduct should not be applied at work. How? Consider the supervisor who embarrasses or shames an employee who objects to deceptive sales practices. "You're in sales, not the priesthood!" the supervisor might snarl as peers look on with interest. Manipulative supervisors might try to banish important felt emotions (Step 3), like fear or guilt. For example, a mortgage lender's justified fears about a borrower's poor credit may be allayed by assurances that a default on the loan "will be somebody else's problem." Emotional tyrants may express, or fail to express, moral emotions (Step 5) in ways that actually discourage moral behavior. For example, they may fail to express remorse when they cause harm to others, dismissing such behavior as "just business." Remorse is an acknowledgment to the larger moral community of wrongful behavior and its performance reinforces moral codes for perpetrators and victims (Waldron and Kelley, 2008). Emotional tyrants may reveal contempt for employees who value fairness to customers over profits or they may express glee at the misfortunes of rivals. These emotional displays may have a desensitizing, coarsening effect on the moral sensitivities of coworkers and the climate of the larger organization.

146

Emotional weaponry: a brief primer

The first weapon of an emotional tyrant is the language of emotion. Taking advantage of societal and organizational norms that discourage, and even belittle, some kinds of emotional displays, they set out to hurt others with labels. In essence, they are manipulating the emotions of co-workers by using emotion-laden language, often with a larger audience in mind. When my working students describe their experiences on the job, I see that they sometimes are the victims (and the perpetrators) of this brand of verbal aggression. The derogatory labels include "cry baby," "emotional trainwreck," "bitchy," "hopeless," "bloodless bastard," "scaredy cat," "grump-meister," "drama queen," "hard-hearted," "Debbie downer," and a host of other colorful, sometimes silly, but apparently hurtful appellations. Often the tyrant "scores points" with peers, by associating others with emotional qualities that are devalued at work. Of course, the recipient is often able to discount these efforts, but when an audience of peers is present, often feelings of embarrassment, hurt, or shame are the result. The tyrant contrasts negatively the emotional behavior of his or her victims with the praiseworthy emotional displays of more "professional" peers. In a striking example, one which may be interpreted as a kind of occupational bravado, a fighter pilot from the US Air Force belittled the crying response of a fellow flyer who, during a training flight, witnessed the fiery and fatal crash of his friend's jet. The emotional response was preserved on the cockpit voice recorder. "We were embarrassed," the pilot told me in an interview. "I mean, nobody wants their friend to die. But geeze, you don't *cry* about it. Not if you want to be a pilot" (Waldron, 1994: 388).

A second way that emotional tyrants inflict harm is through the use of emotional communication tactics. A selection of these is presented in table 5.2 (expanded from Waldron, 2009: 19). For example, in emotional *betrayal,* a co-worker's "secret" emotions are inappropriately shared with third parties, or emotional commitments are undermined. An example might be the revelation that a co-worker has been feeling dissatisfied with supervision or envious of another co-worker. *Deflection* is an effort to dodge

Table 5.2 Tactics of Emotional Tyrannists with Discourse Examples

Tactic	Exemplar
Appropriation	"After weeks of not listening to our complaints, the administration acted like they had been deeply concerned from the beginning. It was like, 'Oh, we feel your pain.' Which was B.S., cause they never gave a *&%!"
Betraying	"I put my heart into the job because my boss liked me and believed in me. But after he got promoted I got nothing but coldness. He stabbed me in the heart."
Blackmailing	"I (stupidly) told my boss about a crush I had on a co-worker. He threatened to tell if I didn't show a good attitude. Maybe joking . . . but he enjoyed the threat."
Cutting	"She would stare at you with dagger eyes and say something snarky. She wanted to cut you down and make you feel small."
Deflecting	"He basically told us it was not his fault [that people haven't been paid on time]. We all should be mad at the contractor. He dodged responsibility."
Discounting	"[the Dean asked], Why did you care so much about the staff evaluations? All I care about is the faculty. We really don't need to be so emotional."
Embarrassing	"She criticized me right on the floor, in front of my customers (two were my friends)! My face went red and I ran for the bathroom."
Faking	"The HR person could really pretend like she was sincere when we brought up a grievance. Like she cared and was all worried. But it was an act, a joke really."
Flattering	"He was a major brown-noser, always kissing up and being nice."
Grinding	"After a while I got tired of the everyday anger control issues. She snipped and yelled and wore me down over time. I finally left (which is what she wanted)."
Guilting	"Because I was super-dedicated back then, they could guilt me into anything. I'd stay late because they would make me feel disloyal or selfish for going home."
Intimidating	"I was told I would pay a huge price if I went public with the problem. Basically, they scared me into conformity."
Exhorting	"[My boss] was like a preacher at church, getting us all whooped up and excited about the company and our sales. But we found out it was all BS. The company didn't care

Table 5.2 (continued)

Tactic	Exemplar
	about us and the bosses made all of the money. We were used."
Orchestrating	"This guy (team leader) was threatened by me. So he went around spreading rumors that I wasn't working hard and thought I was too good to work. Before I knew it people resented me."
Reframing	"You think poor sales are no big deal? This is an embarrassment to me."
Ridiculing	"When I see my servers cry, I know they aren't ready for prime time. Crying doesn't make customers happy and babies don't get tips. I say, buck-up!"
Shaming	"After I complained, they made me feel like I was being selfish, like I was more important than everybody. Just because I wanted them to follow the [curriculum development] process rather than just rush it through."
Silencing	[A colleague told me] "Sure I am disgusted . . . and I think the policy is stupid. But keep my name out of it. I have already had my head chewed off in too many meetings (by university administrators)."
Vanquishing	"Wipe that smile off your face and don't let me see it again!"

emotions that one "should" feel, such as guilt, or to redirect emotions to another person. A friend of the author's described a home contractor who refused to feel guilty, despite repeatedly missing construction deadlines. The contractor attempted to convince his increasingly annoyed customers to direct their wrath at suppliers or other customers who took too much of his time. *Discounting* is a tactic used to devalue the emotions of employees. During a stint in administration, the author was advised by a dean not to "care so much" about members of the administrative staff because it was the faculty that really mattered at the university. More aggressive tactics include *grinding down* employees through repeated emotional appeals, *vanquishing* their emotions ("that is nothing to smile about"), *cutting* them down with hurtful comments, and *intimidating* them with threats. Leaders can use their communication to spread emotion across the workforce in ways that are harmful. *Exhorting* is the process of "whooping up" emotions, sometimes under false pretenses. A student of the author once described being misled by a supervisor at her restaurant who "fired up" the employees for a holiday weekend by pledging that by working long hours on Friday and Saturday, they would earn the right to schedule the most desirable shifts the next week. She described being deflated and disappointed when the promise wasn't kept, allegedly because upper management squelched the deal. Some employees are disenfranchised by the tactic of *orchestrating*, an often clandestine effort by a rival to cultivate feelings of jealousy or resentment toward a victim. Others are the target of *flattering*, a deceptive effort to create feelings of affection and goodwill for the sole purpose of personal gain.

The tactics of emotional tyrants are often used in combination, with one following upon another. And, of course, the effects on employees are compounded as time passes and they grow weary of the abuse. I previously offered this observation about a situation that developed at my own university, which demonstrates the sometimes absurd lengths to which management will go in attempting to manipulating feelings.

the implementation of a complicated new computer system was by all accounts badly bungled. One unfortunate result was that some (largely low-level) employees received reduced paychecks, or none at all, for several pay cycles. Employees expressed concern, then alarm, then frustration, then anger, and finally burning resentment as their plight went unacknowledged by leaders. After remaining mute about the problem for weeks (*discounting* the emotional urgency expressed by employees and many of their supervisors), the president's office finally responded by blaming the contractor and the human resources department (*deflecting*), claiming that the administration has been highly concerned all along (*appropriation* of employee emotion), and arguing that the administration had "no choice" but to implement the computer change because the old system was defunct and essentially in danger of self-destructing. This last tactic seemed designed to cultivate sympathy for the beleaguered administration. At the same time, administrative rhetoric implied that employees were selfish to complain about their personal losses in light of the organization's imminent destruction at the hands of a decrepit computer. Not surprisingly, this *shaming* tactic was met by considerable indignation at what appeared to be emotional manipulation. (Waldron, 2009: 20)

This last example illustrates that those in charge of organization-wide systems enjoy unique access to, and responsibility for, emotional resources. Although I doubt that any university administrator intended to be an emotional tyrant, the priorities and procedures they implemented certainly had the effect of manipulating employee emotions. Disregarding the previous experiences of other universities, officials chose to implement the new computer system rapidly, with limited pilot testing. In doing so, they failed to anticipate the emotional effects on the workforce – or they may have simply decided that these effects were not important. One can imagine the planners making statements like this: "Well, this is going to upset people for awhile, but let's get it over with". Given this mindset, officials directed few resources to preparing employees for the disruptive effects or listening for their emotional responses. This emotionally tone-deaf approach persisted, even when employees became quite anguished. Indeed, as employees grew enraged by shrunken paychecks and the prospect of missed mortgage payments, they turned to an external website to vent their frustrations. Supervisors who expressed indignation on behalf of employees were labeled "complainers," told to be patient, or simply received no response whatsoever. Finally, a private credit union stepped into the breech and offered low-cost loans to distressed employees. Only well after the crises had passed did the president finally offer a small amount of cash (reported to be $25.00) as compensation for employees who had been most affected. Predictably, employees responded with ridicule and disgust. This extended example demonstrates that emotional manipulation is often attributable to the systems created by powerful persons, rather than their personal communications.

Management control of internal and external messages provides another opportunity for the exercise of emotional tyranny.

Referring again to the university example, messages from the administration framed employee responses in ways that devalued their emotions and advanced the administration's version of events. Employees were characterized as ungrateful and churlish children; in contrast, the administration was taking heroic action and making painful decisions that would save the organization from ruin. When they (finally) responded to employee anger, administrators might have expressed empathy or even remorse. These emotional displays would have signaled that, despite the unfortunate circumstances, leaders were sensitive to injustices experienced by employees and aware of the human toll exacted by a massive organizational change.

The organization also controls messages shared with external audiences, and, interestingly, the university touted its rapid adoption of the computer system to the business community and cultivated coverage from the business press. Indeed, its chief technology officer was hailed in a major business newspaper for the success of the effort. These observations reveal that emotional manipulation arises in part from an organization's efforts to please multiple audiences with different kinds of emotional portrayals. At my university, the administration takes great pride in its "business-like" approach to education. It is important that university leaders be portrayed as confident innovators, swashbuckling deal-makers, and courageous visionaries. This identity is incompatible with certain other emotional capacities associated with leadership, such as empathy for employees, the ability to remain calm in the face of emotional dissent, or a healthy fear of the consequences of risky organizational actions. Indeed, these latter qualities would be difficult for the university's PR staff to package in a press release, but they may have helped administrators avoid what, for many of the least powerful employees, became an emotionally exhausting debacle.

Conclusion: Emotion as a Guide to Doing Good

In this chapter, I have argued that certain kinds of emotional communications are essential in weaving the moral fabric of an organization. The moral emotions provide the hues to this complicated tapestry. Some are vivid and others dull, some are pleasing and others jarring, but they all contribute to the very human experience that is work. Communication, in its various forms, is the weaving process, binding employees together with formal and informal codes of conduct. These moral ties are stitched together, frayed, and repaired, using such tools as emotion words, communication tactics, and the messages organizations produce in response to emotional situations. Role requirements, organizational and societal values, and workplace procedures serve as the framework around which the fabric is constructed. Although the process is rarely intentional or fully understood, leaders and members forge the moral character of their working lives from these raw materials.

Returning to a theme introduced in chapter 1, I leave this chapter with a final thought. Emotions humanize organizations. But, more than that, by communicating emotions we make our workplaces more humane. By expressing admiration, we provide vital acknowledgment to those who do their best for us and our employer. In communicating compassion, we help those who have been victimized by unfortunate circumstance or uncharitable colleagues. By editing displays of anger, we allow others to feel safe around us. In voicing feelings of remorse, we acknowledge wrongdoing and signal a willingness to make things right. I have presented many examples in this chapter of the ways in which emotional communication can be a tool of those bent on wrongdoing, but I hope the reader has noticed that the moral emotions help us recognize and cultivate that which is right. In that sense, emotion is a guide to doing good.

References

Armon-Jones, C. (1986). The social functions of emotions. In R. Harre (ed.), *The Social Construction of Emotion*. Oxford: Blackwell, pp. 57–82.

Averhill, J. R. (1983). Studies on anger and aggression. *American Psychologist*, 38: 1145–60.

Bies, R. J. (1987). The predicament of injustice: the management of moral outrage. In L. L. Cummings and B. M. Staw (eds), *Research in*

Organizational Behavior, Volume 9. Greenwich, CT: JAI Publishers, pp. 289–319.

Coupland, C., Brown, A. D., Daniels, K., and Humphreys, M. (2008). Saying it with feeling: analysing speakable emotions. *Human Relations*, 61: 327–53.

Darwin, C. ([1872] 1998). *The Expression of the Emotions in Man and Animals* (3rd edn). London: HarperCollins.

Fineman, S. (ed.). (2000). *Emotion in Organizations* (2nd edn). London: Sage.

Freud, S. (1961). Inhibitions, symptoms, and anxiety. In J. Strachey (ed. And trans.), *The Standard Edition of the Complete Psychological Works of Sigmund Freud* (vol. 20). London: Hogarth, pp 77–176 (original work published 1926).

Goffman, E. (1955). On facework. *Psychiatry*, 18: 215–36.

Haidt, J. (2003). The moral emotions. In R. J. Davidson, K. R. Scherer, and H. H. Goldsmith (eds), *Handbook of Affective Sciences*. Oxford: Oxford University Press, pp. 852–70.

Harlos, K. P., and Pinder, C. C. (2000). Emotion and injustice in the workplace. In S. Fineman (ed.), *Emotion in Organizations* (2nd edn). London: Sage, pp. 255–76.

Hochschild, A. (1983). *The Managed Heart*. Berkeley, CA: University of California Press.

James, W. (1884). What is an emotion? *Mind*, 9: 188–205.

Kassing, J. (2007). Going around the boss: exploring the consequences of circumvention. *Management Communication Quarterly*, 21: 55–75.

Keltner, D. (2009). *Born To Be Good: The Science of a Meaningful Life*. New York: W. W. Norton & Company.

Lazarus, R. S. (1984). On the primacy of cognition. *American Psychologist*, 39: 124–9.

Planalp, S. (1999). *Communicating Emotion: Social, Moral, and Political Processes*. Cambridge: Cambridge University Press.

Sharkey, W. F. (1997). "Why would anyone want to intentionally embarrass me?" In R. Kowalski (ed.), *Aversive Interpersonal Behaviors*. New York: Plenum Press, pp 57–90.

Solomon, R. C. (1989). The emotions of injustice. *Social Justice Research*, 3: 345–74.

Waldron, V. (1994). Once more, *with feeling*: reconsidering the role of emotion in work. *Communication Yearbook 17*. Thousand Oaks, CA: Sage Publications, pp. 388–416.

Waldron V. (2009). Emotional tyranny at work: suppressing the moral emotions. In P. Lutgen-Sandvik and B. Davenport-Sypher (eds), *Destructive Organizational Communication: Processes, Consequences, and Constructive Ways of Organizing*. New York: Routledge, pp. 9–26.

Waldron, V., and Kelley, D. (2008). *Communicating Forgiveness*. Newbury Park, CA: Sage Publications.

Waldron, V., and Krone, K. J. (1991). The experience and expression of emotion in the workplace: a study of a corrections organization. *Management Communication Quarterly*, 4: 287–309.

Waldron, V., Foreman, C., and Miller, R. (1993). Managing gender conflicts in the supervisory relationship: relationship definition strategies used by women and men. In G. Kreps (ed.), *Sexual Harassment: Communication Implications*. Cresskill, NJ: Hammond Press

Weiner, B. (2006). *Social Motivation, Justice, and the Moral Emotions: An Attributional Approach*. Mahwah, NJ: Lawrence Erlbaum Associates.

Zajonc, R. (1984). On the primacy of affect. *American Psychologist*, 39: 117–23.

6

Emotional Trends

In this concluding chapter, I invite the reader to explore emerging and interesting trends at the intersections of organizational and emotional life. Among the issues considered is the increased *emotional connectivity* that stems from the central role of communication technologies and social media in the lives of workers. I also examine *ephemeral emotion*, the kinds experienced by a new wave of temporary employees with their fleeting connections to co-workers. *Emotional jobs and services* are analyzed with a particular emphasis on career trends and the role of emerging technologies in facilitating emotional communication tasks. *Emotional costs* are considered, with particular reference to the changing economic conditions and the ways that organizations will (and should) respond to them. I suggest that the emotional health of laid-off workers, remaining employees, and their communities should be of greater concern. *Emotional desensitization* is another theme of this final chapter. I examine how it is cultivated, for better or worse, by exposure to such popular media as video games, reality TV, and shows like *The Office*. The growing importance of *emotional mending* is the final topic. Although hurt and wrongdoing seem to be inevitable experiences over the course of a career, I propose workplace forgiveness as a hopeful alternative to revenge and alienation. In the conclusion to this chapter, and the book, I discuss emerging possibilities for *emotional fulfillment* and trace what appears to be a renewed desire for workplaces to also be communities. I revisit the idea first presented in chapter

1, that emotional communication, particularly of the "positive" emotions, is essential to the creation of fulfilling, healthy, and just organizations.

Emotional Connectivity

Communication technologies continue to emerge and morph in ways that will shape emotional experiences at work. Smartphones, Facebook, traditional email, Twitter, electronic calendaring devices, Linked-In, and a host of other technologies serve as emotional umbilical cords, nourishing employees with a continuous flow of messages. One obvious implication is that workers are more emotionally connected to their jobs, co-workers, and customers for ever-longer periods; for some, the expectation is that they will be available 24 hours a day. As this trend progresses, it is likely that more employees find themselves in a near constant state of emotional arousal as they anticipate, seek, process, and respond to the next tweet or text. The emotions of a work day can more easily follow them home in the form of a continuing stream of electronic nudges. Many workers find themselves perched over a laptop before they retire to bed. What are they doing? Often they are performing emotional communication tasks: calming down after-hours crises, adding their "two bits" to heated email conversations among co-workers, or composing tactful responses to the requests of an upset boss.

One interesting aspect of 24-hour connectivity is its blurring of work and what traditionally has been considered leisure time. Leisure serves a variety of potentially restorative functions, but surely one of these is the creation of positive emotional experiences that are not available at work. Employees spend their leisure time in myriad ways – quietly at home with family, wildly riding a Ferris wheel at the local amusement park, catching fish with a lure, puttering in a garden, a relaxed day at the spa, or traveling to visit friends in distant places. Each activity strikes different emotional tones: calming conversation; an exhilarating loss of control; joy at the tug of a fish; quiet wonder at the beauty of roses; emotional nurturance; the rekindled warmth of friendships renewed.

Increasingly, though, workers are finding it difficult, maybe even frowned upon, to be disconnected from work during vacations and weekends. And some of us, deeply dependent on our communication technologies, find it unpleasant to go "cold turkey," by leaving the laptop at home during a week's vacation or turning off the BlackBerry for the weekend. The resulting integration of work and leisure even has a name: "weisure time" (Conley, 2009; Patterson, 2009). The trend may reflect the increasing number of hours that professional workers spend on their jobs. They just find it difficult to get their work done during traditional working hours. And, as Conley notes, it may also reflect that, for many people, work has become more fun. For them, leisure is *woven into* work, when they play online games during down moments, chat with their Facebook friends in between work-related emails, or peek at an amusing YouTube video during a quick coffee break. Of course, even for traditional employees, a certain amount of leisure time has been spent, by choice, with co-workers. The issue now is whether technology has tethered people in a more or less conscious way to their jobs and their colleagues and, if so, is the evolving nature of work placing strictures on their emotional lives?

Extreme levels of connectivity can leave workers feeling exhilarated, innervated, or emotionally drained. It speeds up the emotional processing cycle – feelings are more quickly expressed and responded to. But it may also crowd out or distort the emotional communication that sustains personal relationships. Will hyper-connected employees miss signals of emotional distress displayed by children or spouse? Will they become irritable at minor provocations? When a family crisis arises, will they be too "tapped out" to offer compassionate assistance? In sum, can employees who are electronically tethered to their jobs, disconnect long enough, and well enough, to manage the emotional complexities of face-to-face relationships? Much has been written in recent years about the possibility that excessive dependency on Internet tools (e.g., Google) could be making people cognitively "dumber" (e.g., Carr, 2010). Might it also be making us emotionally duller?

These questions might represent over-the-top handwringing. Technology-mediated emotion is nothing new. After all, it was more than 100 years ago that the telephone made it possible for distant family members to share their joys and sorrows immediately rather than in the delayed communications of personal letters. Of course, the slower pace of letter writing had then, and has now, certain emotional benefits. Slower-paced communication, like slower-paced eating, allows us to savor the flavors of our relationships. In taking our time, we think more deeply, share more feelings, use language to make finer distinctions. Consider this letter from Thomas Jefferson to John Adams, with whom he worked to write the declaration of independence. The colleagues became lifelong friends, although the relationship was at times strained by political differences. They lived hundreds of miles apart, a distance that could be crossed on horseback or by letter. Late in their lives, after years of regular correspondence, Jefferson learned that his colleague's beloved wife, Abigail, had died. This is what he wrote to describe his emotions on learning of that sad event:

MONTICELLO, November 13, 1818.
The public papers, my dear friend, announce the fatal event of which your letter of October the 20th had given me ominous foreboding. Tried myself in the school of affliction, by the loss of every form of connection which can rive the human heart, I know well, and feel what you have lost, what you have suffered, are suffering, and have yet to endure. The same trials have taught me that for ills so immeasurable, time and silence are the only medicine. I will not, therefore, by useless condolences, open afresh the sluices of your grief, nor, although mingling sincerely my tears with yours, will I say a word more where words are vain, but that it is of some comfort to us both, that the term is not very distant, at which we are to deposit in the same cerement, our sorrows and suffering bodies, and to ascend in essence to an ecstatic meeting with the friends we have loved and lost, and whom we shall still love and never lose again. God bless you and support you under your heavy affliction.

Jefferson's reflective prose reveals his deep familiarity with afflictions that "rive the human heart" with grief. He is both empathetic and sympathetic, but he refrains from useless condolences that can open afresh the sluices of grief. He offers comfort in the form of hope, his wish that their own certain deaths shall be an "ecstatic meeting" of friends. It is hard to imagine Jefferson's sentiments being expressed in a tweet or posted on a Facebook wall. On the other hand, such technologies would have helped the former presidents exchange the sad news more quickly. Jefferson's message is powerful because he took the time to write about his feelings; to consider fully the nuanced human experience that is his friend's grief. The kinds of emotional connection forged and maintained by their stream of letters makes the relationship of Adams and Jefferson rich, personal, and unique. I am not suggesting that these kinds of communication should be replicated by modern-day colleagues. But I am suggesting that some technologies, unless used judiciously, cultivate only the most tenuous and shallow of emotional bonds.

Fortunately, it appears companies are becoming more attuned to the way that work arrangements can fray, or sustain, the web of emotional connections that support employees over the long term. Consulting firm Deloitte is apparently one of these (Fitzpatrick, 2010).

> On the worst days, Chris Keehn used to go 24 hours without seeing his daughter with her eyes open. A soft spoken tax accountant in Deloitte's downtown Chicago office, he hated saying no when she asked for a ride to preschool. By November he had enough. "I realized I could control this, he says with a small shrug . . . In January, Keehn started telecommuting four days a week, and when Kathryn, 4, starts T-ball this summer, he will be sitting along the baseline. (p. 45)

Deloitte has replaced the metaphor of the career ladder with the notion of a "lattice," which allows employees to progress through their career by climbing laterally along continuously adjusted paths. Employees can request adjustments in their work schedules and tasks, dialing back or throttling up their degree of investment in work. The result is a system that allows employees to periodically redirect more of their emotional energy to parenting, caretaking, and other commitments. Some organizations view these kinds of arrangements as economically wise, as well as emotionally healthy. An example from the public sector is the US Patent and Trademark Office (USPTO), which in 2007 reported that roughly 40 percent of its workforce engaged in some form of telecommuting, saving roughly $1.7 million in fuel costs (USPTO, 2007). From these examples, it is clear that workplace trends are altering the degree to which workers are emotionally connected to their colleagues and their families. Some of these trends are good for people and their organizations. Others have the potential to cause emotional harm. Certainly, the degree to which work nurtures or inhibits emotional connections will be of increasing concern as technology continues to evolve.

Ephemeral Emotional Connections

A significant number of US workers have temporary or "contingent" relationships with their employers. In its 2005 Current Population Survey, the US Bureau of Labor Statistics (2005) reported that roughly 11.7 percent of the working population was employed in contingent roles. They were independent contractors (7.4 percent), on-call workers (1.8 percent), "temp agency" hires (0.9 percent), or contracted from another organization on a "per-project" basis (0.6 percent). At the time of this writing, those numbers may be increasing due to poor economic conditions which make employers reluctant to make more permanent arrangements. By forging temporary relationships with workers, organizations avoid long-term financial commitments and respond more nimbly to changing economic conditions (for a thorough review, see Kunda, Barley, and Evans, 2002). For some workers, these temporary arrangements work well. Those who possess sought-after technical skills are well paid and some enjoy the variety that comes with their changing work situations (Sullivan, 1999). These "free agents" are temporary workers by choice.

Table 6.1 Some reasons for temporary work

Reasons	Example/description
Skill development	Gaining practice with a software program; using temporary work to build job skills
Trial period	Demonstrating value for a possible permanent hire
Family flexibility	Preserving flexibility for caretaking or parenting
Education	Students use temporary work to fund their education
Health	Working when health limitations allow
Free agency	Choosing jobs which maximize income or satisfaction
Supplemental work	Temporary jobs supplement a permanent job
Variety/boredom	Worker prefers variety in working conditions
Only option	No permanent work is available

However, the reasons for temporary work vary considerably. Table 6.1 describes the more common ones. Some workers take impermanent assignments to supplement the income from a permanent job, to establish their credentials for permanent employment, or because they become bored in long-term positions. Several of my graduate students work as substitute teachers when their class schedule allows and they need quick cash to pay their bills. For many others, temporary work is the only option. They make themselves available as contractors or hire out through temporary employment agencies because permanent jobs are unavailable in their career field or in their geographic area. This may be particularly true when the worker's occupational prospects are constricted by downsizing, mergers, or the replacement of human workers with labor-saving technologies.

One might guess that temporary arrangements are most emotionally satisfying when workers choose the arrangement. But, as a recent study of 623 Belgian workers revealed (de Cuyper and de Witte, 2008), the picture is not so clear. They found that measures of volition were largely uncorrelated with measures of job satisfaction and workers' commitment. A complicating factor is the measurement of volition, the degree to which temporary work is chosen. In a poor economy, when permanent jobs are few, prospective employees may have "no choice" but to take temporary

162

jobs as a way to build their résumé and increase chances for a permanent job. However, the decision to do so feels like a choice – an active effort to adapt to less-than-ideal conditions. Similarly, a person may choose a temporary role (e.g., as a substitute school teacher) due to health limitations. Perhaps he or she can work only on "good" days. But a person in this situation might prefer other options, such as non-teaching positions or part-time permanent work, that are unavailable. In addition to this conceptual ambiguity, some temporary workers report high levels of emotional commitment to their "unchosen" jobs, perhaps because they view them as a welcome opening to permanent employment. From the literature on contingent work arrangements, it is easy to see how organizations benefit. For employees, the benefits and costs are filtered through a screen comprised of their unique personal situations and goals.

Contingent relationships affect emotional communication in a variety of ways. This may be most evident in relationship management practices. As discussed in chapter 4, relationship maintenance is the kind of communication that sustains and stabilizes a relationship over long periods of time. The process might be less important in temporary relationships. When faced with a temporary colleague, permanent workers may be reluctant to invest effort in such maintenance behaviors as asking questions about family life, sharing personal stories, offering amusing anecdotes, or expressing emotional support. Supervisors may see little value in mentoring, sharing "inside" information, or informally chatting with a temporary worker. Instead, these relationships are likely to be maintained more formally, by filing reports or attending required meetings.

Temporary workers might be more emotionally cautious in some cases, because their lack of relational history (and job protections) makes them vulnerable to easy termination. If they hope to obtain permanent work, contingent employees may feel pressure to suppress negative feelings and display positive ones. However, "temps" with highly desired skills might be less likely to regulate their emotional displays because their employment options are many and their commitment is limited. Perhaps they are more likely to "tell off" an overbearing boss or give voice to their feelings of dissatisfaction.

Temporary work can leave employees feeling lonely or emotionally alienated. In such cases, ephemeral connections with co-workers might be supplemented by more lasting kinds of connection, as shown in this case.

"Sandy," a skilled user of geographic mapping software, works from home on a contract basis. Companies hire her for weeks or months, and during that period she makes occasional visits to their offices or connects with her new co-workers at coffee shops to discus project details over lattes and laptops. Sandy cherishes the freedom of her work-at-home life. But she struggles with feelings of loneliness and misses her old job, where she shared a storefront office with an unruly but gregarious gang of software developers. Sandy told me that she feels a quick thrill when her computer beeps – a signal that one of her temporary co-workers has sent her an IM or email. She describes her work as "emotional starvation" and wonders if she is becoming too dependent on her domestic partner for the emotionally satisfying conversations she has come to crave. In response, she has expanded her social network by becoming more active in a faith community and volunteering with a local group of environmental activists. This new kind of "work" puts her in the midst of passionate people who are often in conflict, but she finds it a refreshing tonic to the emotional distance that characterizes her regular job.

It is clear that temporary work can be a good thing. If nothing else, it allows some employees to remain only briefly in emotionally toxic workplaces. Contingent employees may foster more permanent emotional connections with peers by becoming active in professional associations or alumni groups. Even under temporary conditions, it is possible to forge satisfying relationships with peers that can be maintained after the job terminates. Social media make these kinds of relationships viable and potentially rewarding. Rather than being joined by proximity and a shared organization, workers can be connected by technology and a common community of online friends. In short, it is possible to supplement ephemeral emotional connections with ones that could become more permanent.

Emotional Jobs, Products, and Services

In the hit movie *Up in the Air,* actor George Clooney travels the country performing some of the most emotionally intensive communication imaginable. Clooney's character is known for his unique skill set – the ability to inform people that their jobs will be terminated and their services are no longer needed by their organization. In what might be labeled *emotion outsourcing,* organizations delegate this delicate work to an outside expert; in this case, one who is adept at delivering emotionally distressing messages. Clooney models the process for his young sidekick, demonstrating how to deliver the bad news gently but firmly, read the signs of employees' emotional distress, absorb their anger, and firmly direct attention to the possibilities for a more hopeful future. Unimpressed, she proposes a model for delivering the service via teleconference, a communication method that proves to be efficient but tragically impersonal.

Emotional jobs

The movie illustrates, although not with complete realism, just one of the many forms of emotionally intensive work that is becoming more common in the US workforce. Employee termination is more likely a job performed by in-house staff. But it is often contracted out to counselors and job-transition specialists who help employees deal with the emotional aftermath of job loss. Indeed, organizations are increasingly outsourcing human resources functions. Among industries, employment services are predicted in a recent United States Bureau of Labor Statistics Report (2010a) to have the fifth-fastest growth rate between now and 2018. From the report, it is clear that some other high-growth occupations centrally involve emotional communication.

Projections indicate that no industry will grow jobs faster than healthcare, which is projected to grow 21 percent as consumers come to expect more expansive services and the aging population requires more care. Doctors, nurses, and a cadre of other healthcare professionals provide invaluable technical expertise, but their success also depends on emotional communication tasks. These include offering assurance to anxious patients, displaying a warm "bedside manner," delivering bad news, using appropriate levels of fear to encourage patient compliance with medical instructions, managing the frustrations of bureaucracy and interdisciplinary teamwork, and cultivating the emotional support that patients need from families.

The government report predicts that the educational services sector will increase by 12 percent or 1.7 million jobs. Teachers at levels from kindergarten to college must be adept at recognizing the emotional cues of their students and at keeping them emotionally engaged. For many college teachers, the job will increasingly involve technology. How do we make emotional connections with students who we know only through their online identities? What emotional competencies are we to teach students who maintain their relationships through texts and instant messaging? Other questions are variations on those we have been asking for a long time. Are students prepared for the emotional demands of intensive teamwork? Are they ready to encounter the emotional practices of co-workers from unfamiliar cultures?

Another area of steep increase is that of community and social services occupations. Human services professionals are trained to be responsive to the needs of distressed populations, the poor, the elderly, and those in need of counseling and emotional support. This industry is expected to expand by 16 percent (448,400 jobs), as mental and behavioral health services are increasingly covered by insurance and the population ages. Employment rates in a number of other communication-intensive professions are expected to increase at least modestly. These include public relations, audience opinion research, advertising, and jobs related to development of social media and communication technologies. These jobs all involve assessment and management of audience responses to emotional messages in various communication channels.

Jobs in retail sales will increase more slowly than in the past but, at a projected rate of 4 percent growth, this huge sector will add 654,000 more workers. As discussed previously in chapters 1 and 3, retail sales is the site of intensive emotional labor, as clerks are required to produce pleasant emotional displays and manage with aplomb those situations in which customers are dissatisfied or emotionally demanding. Other providers of emotionally skilled services to the public will increase at substantial rates as well, including emergency responders, home-healthcare aides, financial services and insurance specialists, and various kinds of salespersons.

Emotional products and services

The communication of emotion continues to be a challenging task for many people. New products and services are helping individuals and organizations perform more competently. This trend is accelerating for several reasons. First is the continuing recognition of the importance of emotional intelligence, emotional communication competence, and related individual qualities. Entrepreneurs recognize that people will welcome products that redress perceived weaknesses in these areas (see Fineman, 2000, on the commodification of emotion). Second, as noted above, emotional dexterity will only increase in its centrality to certain kinds of work, particularly in industries that are expected to grow. In these sectors of the economy, organizations will seek competitive advantage by improving the quality and efficiency of emotional communication. Finally, the trend toward automating previously face-to-face aspects of communication is likely to accelerate. Current examples include online matchmaking services, electronic meetings, social networking sites, interactive games, and online job application systems.

What are some examples of these evolving products and services? Consider ToneCheck™, a downloadable software program that is promoted on its website (<http://tonecheck.com>) with this message:

Studies show e-mail messages are interpreted incorrectly 50% of the time. ToneCheck™ is an e-mail plug-in that flags sentences with words or phrases that may convey unintended emotion or tone, then helps you re-write them. Just like Spell Check . . . but for Tone. Avoid continuous editing and unnecessary conflict with ToneCheck™.

This product automates a process that emotionally competent communicators perform intuitively: imagining the emotional reactions of their audience and adjusting the message accordingly. One can imagine a similar system based on voice recognition, perhaps as an application for a smartphone. When your voice reveals undesirable levels of certain emotions, let's say you are becoming too angry during a conversation with a co-worker or sounding too cowed during negotiations with an aggressive supplier, your phone would let you know, and, perhaps, modulate the emotional tone of the message. These kinds of devices could be useful in training workers who must strike the right emotional tone in their interactions, including nurses, police officers, and telemarketers.

Not surprisingly, the ability to recognize emotions based on universally recognizable facial expressions (see chapter 2) has commercial implications. Pattern recognition software is being developed to scan crowds and locate persons who appear to be disgusted, fearful, or angry. When refined, these programs might be used for security purposes at border crossings or airports. Companies and universities are promoting the promise of their research on these systems (e.g., Concordia University, 2008). Helping people assess their own emotions is another area of product development. Gavin de Becker is a well-known security specialist and author of a series of popular books on assessing and preventing violence, including *The Gift of Fear* (1997). De Becker argues that fear is a "gift" in the sense that it alerts us to danger and tunes us to our self-protective intuitive responses. In recent years he has developed a series of tools under the name of *Mosaic* for measuring the violence potential of a co-worker, student, or domestic partner (<https://www.mosaicmethod.com/>). De Becker's work is grounded in a variety of observational skills, and some of them involve recognizing differences in emotion.

When is a domestic partner's persistent questioning an expression of concern and when does it signal the controlling behavior of a would-be batterer? When is a co-worker simply letting off steam and when is it a foreshadowing of workplace violence? The success of these and other commercial methods of threat assessment are difficult to ascertain, but they seem to be growing in popularity in a culture where incidents of violent crime, terrorism, and workplace violence receive high levels of media attention.

Of course, a whole host of familiar and emerging technologies add emotional depth to the messages created for customers and co-workers. Podcasts are richer in emotional cues than traditional print endorsements if you want your prospective customers to "hear" the enthusiastic endorsement of current customers. Emoticons of various types allow Facebook communications and even traditional emails to convey emotional meanings to co-workers. But these communication tools are clunky compared to new applications like the Flipboard for iPad (<http://www.flipboard.com/>), a personalized "social magazine" which allows you to integrate a whole host of communication features (picture sharing, Twitter feeds, blogs, podcasts, steaming media, social networks) in one highly attractive set of screens. The immediacy and rich audio-visual features of Flipboard increase the capacity of users to share emotions in real time.

Clearly, a host of new digital tools will alter the emotional landscape of work. The various processes and functions of emotional communication that have been reviewed in earlier chapters can be imitated and aided as technologies evolve. These changes won't always improve on the processes we use now; some may even be poor imitators of the face-to-face processes they replace. In some cases, these innovations will be used for exploiting rather than improving the lives of workers. However, as I argued in chapter 1, emotional communication plays an integral role in facilitating cooperation in complex organizations. By aiding that process, emerging products and services have the potential to do much good.

Economic Trends and Emotional Costs

As discussed in chapter 1, the emotional implications of work flow across the permeable boundaries of organizations. Recall that Alejandra, the successful science teacher, experienced some of her emotions in reaction to social and economic forces that shaped her job and her school. These included the occupational expectations that she had internalized, a new cultural preference for test-based measures of learning, and the socio-economic forces that may have discouraged parents from being directly involved in their children's education. Alejandra struggled to integrate family and work roles, a balancing act that is complicated by cultural expectations about the emotional contributions that should be made by men and women (Kelan, 2008). She realized that these larger trends were exacting an increasingly costly emotional toll. Researchers have tracked workers like Alejandra from home to work and work to home (Judge, Ilies, and Scott, 2005). For many of them, conflicts experienced in one realm have emotional consequences in the other. When a worker's life becomes more emotionally taxing due to economic or cultural change, families and co-workers serve an important buffering function. But they also assume new emotional costs.

Recently, the newspapers, websites, and airwaves were eagerly covering the saga of an airline attendant whose story might have been drafted from the pages of Arlie Hochschild's classic work on emotional labor, *The Managed Heart*. Steven Slater had served airline passengers for years before he finally reached his emotional breaking point. Then, according to news reports, a passenger who had been unusually obnoxious since boarding the flight apparently struck the attendant in the head as he slammed shut the overhead luggage compartment (Mayerowitz, 2010). The stunned attendant waited until the flight had landed before he commandeered the loudspeaker and berated the unruly passenger with a stream of expletives. He then purportedly grabbed a beer from the galley, released the jet's inflatable emergency evacuation ramp, and launched himself out of the plane and into the annals of customer-service infamy.

As analysts offered their comments and talk-show hosts fielded phone calls from airline passengers and attendants, a consensus seemed to emerge. Steven Slater's grandiose exit was a predictable response to the rudeness and emotional abuse that increasingly define the work of airline attendants. These emotional laborers are on the front lines of several social and economic trends. Airlines are squeezing in more passengers, reducing services, and increasing fees in response to economic pressures. Fears of terrorism and economic anxieties are keeping passengers on edge. As the primary point of customer contact, the flight attendant is increasingly the target of dehumanizing hostility. As Hochschild (1983) suggested decades ago, these and other service employees are incurring serious personal costs due to the continuous emotional demands of their work.

Unfortunately, these emotional costs to employees are sometimes ignored or trivialized as organizations adjust to economic or cultural change. As the example above makes clear, this is nothing new. Emotional reactions to change have always been discounted. Employees are sometimes chided for "taking things too personally" and they are advised to emphasize organizational principles rather than personal costs when they object (Hegstrom, 1999). Of course, the expression of unfiltered emotional reactions can be destructive for employees and their organizations. But, as I proposed in chapters 2 and 5, emotions often signal that something important is going unrecognized. Organizations that trivialize emotional reactions to change may be missing indicators of employees' well-being, their investment in the organization's future, and their misgivings about organizational justice.

What *is* new, and a reflection of larger cultural and economic norms, is the trivialization of the emotional costs *outside* of organizations – costs that are shouldered by families, communities, and government programs. As one example, the number of laid-off workers in the US (and many other countries) has been mounting for several years, as companies respond to shrinking economies. At the time of this writing (August, 2010) roughly 9.5 percent of the US workforce is officially unemployed (United State Bureau of Labor Statistics, 2010a) and many more are underemployed or no longer looking for work. A recent study by the Pew Research Center documents the emotional costs of wide-spread layoffs (Morin and Kochhar, 2010). Data from a random survey of 810 unemployed American adults revealed that 46 percent of respondents who had been unemployed for more than six months experienced strained family relationships, 43 percent lost close friends, 38 percent reported losses in self-esteem, and 25 percent sought counseling for depression or emotional stress. Not surprisingly, it appears that job loss severs employees from important sources of emotional support and has a ripple effect in their family and friendship networks.

Companies provide a number of rationales when they downsize the workforce: seasonal changes in demand for products or services; a contract ended; mergers and reorganizations; work being moved to a cheaper labor market (Levine, 2009). These reasons reflect the interests of managers and shareholders, but they do not reflect the emotional costs to former workers and their communities. Layoffs are unavoidable in some cases, but less emotionally costly options could be considered. The *Wall Street Journal* recently documented steps taken by (mostly small) business owners (Flandez, 2009). Possibilities include job sharing, furloughs, reducing costs, cutting executive compensation, and accepting lower profit margins for the short term.

The emotional distress of unemployment filters back to the workplace. A market researcher at a New York firm was interviewed after an entire division of her firm was eliminated:

> It's depressing . . . You walk into the office and it's quiet, the entire atmosphere is different. When someone gets promoted you want to say, "That's great," but then you realize they got the job because the two other people in that group got laid off; this person was cheaper. You start feeling evil. People say at least you have a job, you should be grateful. Well, I'm not sure how happy I am. And then I feel selfish about that. (Kiviat, 2009)

This employee describes a kind of survivor's guilt, the kid that demoralizes those left behind. Frightened by their own increased odds of termination, just "happy to have a job" – workers who are retained may feel motivated to work harder and sacrifice more for their employer. But other emotional responses are also likely. Survivors may be highly stressed; paralyzed by fear; bitter at the treatment of workers who "deserved better"; disgusted by apparently insensitive leaders who preserved their own interests (and salaries) even as they sacrificed lower-wage employees; more emotionally reactive to adverse events. The disintegration of emotional-support networks inside the organization could leave the workforce feeling dispirited, less cooperative, pessimistic about the future, and emotionally unresponsive. It is these kinds of costs, in addition to the more obvious economic ones, that organizations must consider when deciding how to respond to economic downturns.

Popular Media and Emotional Desensitization

Another developing trend concerns desensitization, the dulling of emotional responsiveness to other people and their circumstances. This phenomenon has been studied for decades as social scientists have documented that repeated exposure to violent media and video games has a desensitizing effect (e.g., Gentile, Lynch, Linder, and Walsh, 2003). Gentile and colleagues observed that a sample of adolescents with high levels of exposure to violence were more likely to shows signs of desensitization as well as behavioral difficulties at school. Given that a larger generation of "gamers" is now entering the workplace, concerns about the increased desensitization seem warranted. Of course, if video games have the potential to effect such changes, they can also be harnessed for the purpose of teaching compassion and cooperative behavior (Chatfield, 2010).

The forces of emotional desensitization extend well beyond the gaming world to other forms of media. Television viewers are repeatedly exposed to ill-tempered emotional displays, public humiliations, and calloused treatment of emotionally vulnerable people. In the US, viewers receive a regular emotional battering from *The People's Court*, and many other instances of courtroom television, in which litigants (including co-workers) make all manner of emotional accusations only to be scolded by judges or shouted down by studio audiences. After careful study, a researcher recently declared these shows "one of the clearest examples of the ritualized celebration of 'negative' emotion in contemporary broadcasting" (Lorenzo-Dus, 2008: 85).

Emotional assault is among the more popular tactics used to capture the attention of a media-saturated audience. Cable television personalities on cable networks such as Fox News or CNBC pile on dubious "evidence" intended to embarrass, shame, or humiliate those with whom they disagree. In another example, reality TV draws viewers by exposing the emotional underbellies of participants. These shows trade on the emotional displays of publicity-hungry "celebrities," overwhelmed parents, hapless bachelorettes, and frazzled "survivors" (for a review, see Escoffery, 2006). Although situations and emotional reactions are actually quite contrived, the audience is invited to mock these people, to scoff at the emotional spectacle, and, perhaps, to assume that emotional displays are simply cheap contrivances that shouldn't be taken seriously. Faced with truly emotional situations at work, these consumers of emotional drama may be ill-prepared to respond.

Some forms of popular media take workplace emotion as their subject. As discussed in chapter 2, these are potential sources of occupational socialization, teaching future and current employees the emotional ropes of (most typically) policing, doctoring, or lawyering. Few are realistic, but some purport to be so. For example, *The Apprentice* features a changing group of eager (if typecast) job applicants vying for the affections of the American tycoon Donald Trump (for an insightful analysis, see Franko, 2006). Trump models his trademark hubris as he "teaches" his acolytes to be fearless capitalists, relatively unhampered by feelings of compassion or humility. Although teamwork is sometimes encouraged, all pretense is put aside when, toward the end of the show, the employees jostle for the boss's attention and make every effort to undermine their peers. Envy, jealousy, *schadenfreude*, and scorn are the emotions that ultimately prevail in *The Apprentice*.

Although viewers of *The Apprentice* presumably watch with

some amusement, other shows make amusement their goal, as they skewer the emotional climate of the workplace. In the US version of *The Office*, a popular "mockumentary," cameras trail the interpersonally clueless Michael Scott and the emotionally discordant interactions of his beleaguered staff of misfits. As a supervisor, Michael is an emotional chameleon, oozing false compassion one moment, erupting in irrational anger the next. Michael manipulates his staff with guilt, humiliates them with inept efforts to recognize their "diversity," and does his utmost to cultivate a climate of envy, jealousy, and adulation for the boss. *The Office* is amusing because it flouts the restrictions that most workers experience. Familiar emotional facades are punctured. Regulated emotions are expressed with impunity. The emotional practices of bullies are held up for ridicule. And in the end, despite it all, compassion often prevails.

The Office is a kind of elixir for the emotional ills of working life. The show's popularity may be evidence of the emotional lunacy that prevails in the workforce, but it makes people laugh about it. It may be that viewers use *The Office* to bolster their own emotional resilience at work – to recognize the sometimes absurd emotional performances required by a job, to find humor in their own circumstances, to know that things could be worse if they worked with Michael Scott. The comedy subjects squirming viewers to scene after scene of embarrassing, over-the-top work-place behavior. In this sense, it emotionally desensitizes them, perhaps in a good way (perhaps not), to the bad behavior they encounter from their own bosses and peers.

Emotional Rampage

No book on workplace emotion can ignore the damage done by emotion run amuck. In August 2010, the news carried word of yet another workplace shooting, this time in Manchester, New Hampshire. Caught stealing from his employer, offered the options of termination or resigning by his own volition, an enraged worker instead chose a gun (Rivera and Robbins, 2010). By the time his violent rampage had ended, eight co-workers and the shooter lay dead. These kinds of high-profile tragedies grab headlines, but rage is expressed more frequently in less deadly ways. Disgruntled employees may seek vengeance through various forms of sabotage (Analoui, 1995). They may break equipment, clog the computer system, or undermine the performance of teammates. Recent research has documented the pervasiveness of these low-level acts of deviance, otherwise known as "insidious workplace behavior" (Greenberg, 2010).

Workplace violence is a serious and complicated topic, one that extends beyond the scope of the current volume. In some cases, employees who are prone to it can be identified through screening and threat assessment methods (see above). Having said that, I would argue that organizations that lack processes for acknowledging and managing extreme emotion are more likely to find it expressed in destructive ways. In my own research, I have heard employees express murderous rage and simmering hate (Waldron, 2000). These feelings can build over time, especially when employees perceive that their options for expressing dissent are limited (see Kassing, 1997). When employees have had enough, they may seek revenge as way of "evening the scales."

Organizations can develop the capacity to head off emotional explosions. Supervisors can be trained to look for signs of emotional distress. As mentioned above, the emotional costs of organizational decisions should be considered alongside economic ones. Employees can be encouraged to seek early intervention when disputes arise among co-workers. Human resource officers can provide structured opportunities for employees to express their feelings of anger or fear. Employees who do so should be protected from retaliation. Deep feelings of resentment spring up when employees perceive management as abusive or believe that the bad behavior of peers will simply be ignored by leaders. My own observations of the sometimes hostile employees of a poorly administered corrections organization convinced me of this truth (Waldron and Krone, 1991). In the years since, it appears that workplace bullying has been increasing (Lutgen-Sandvik, Namie, and Namie, 2009). According to his family, the New Hampshire shooter was harassed by co-workers with racist epithets and a picture of a stick figure hanging by a noose. This kind of bullying is despicable, but it is no excuse for murder. At the same time, it may have triggered violence in an already emotionally volatile employee. Would the incident have been averted if more effort had been expended to identify the signs of emotional distress, stop the harassment, and redress grievances? In this extreme and tragic case, it is difficult to say, but, as a general rule, these kinds of interventions should be well worth the effort.

Emotional Mending: Justice and Forgiveness at Work

Over the life course of a career, it is inevitable that work will lead to damaged relationships, unfair treatment, and deeply hurt feelings. And it goes without saying that organizations can, and sometimes do, engage in wrongful behavior with serious consequences for employees, customers, and communities. As in any human endeavor that requires interdependence and stirs passion, people are hurt by work. Recrimination, relationship termination, a desire for revenge, and grudge-holding are all understandable and justified responses to harm and hurt. But I end this chapter on a positive note, by exploring briefly the notion of forgiveness, a potentially more hopeful and constructive response to workplace transgressions. My colleague Douglas Kelley and I have written more fully on the subject elsewhere (Waldron and Kelley, 2008) and so have other communication scholars (e.g., Metts, Cupach, and Lippert, 2006).

As I discussed in chapter 4, forgiveness processes are ideally designed to hold wrongdoers accountable and they should empower those who have been hurt to seek redress. Parties who participate in the process acknowledge the emotional costs they have paid. They should perceive that the moral values that govern workplace relationships have been acknowledged and restored. Forgiveness can be an interpersonal process, but it has also been implemented at the macro-level, in the process of healing the damage done by institutions (e.g., governments, churches), and between ethnic groups, as in South Africa and Rwanda. Forgiveness processes may be implemented as part of efforts to heal the damage done by organizations to their employees, customers, and communities, although forgiveness alone will never make victims whole.

The details will vary across contexts and with the nature of the transgression, but it can be argued that forgiveness requires the completion of the seven communication tasks listed below. Often the process should be facilitated by a human resources professional, counselor, or interpersonally skilled leader. No person can be compelled to forgive; requiring them to do so would only victimize them again. Indeed, abusive people (and organizations) are often adept at eliciting forgiveness under false pretenses and then repeating the transgression. Caution is warranted. The seven tasks are:

- *Confront the transgression*: The transgressor and the victim should articulate the hurt they have experienced or the wrongdoing that has been committed. This is an opportunity for truth-telling and the process is unlikely to advance until culpability is acknowledged. In some case, both parties share responsibility, and all sides must acknowledge their contributions.
- *Articulate emotion*: The victims articulate their emotional reactions to the offense. These are acknowledged and legitimized by the transgressing party. The emotions are likely to be "re-experienced" later in the process and this step may be repeated.
- *Make sense*: The participants explore the motives for the transgression and reasons why forgiveness should or should not be an option. They develop an understanding of the moral principles that were flouted, relational expectations that were violated, and the losses that were incurred. The parties attempt to see the situation from the other's point of view. They try to be empathetic. Reasons for forgiveness (e.g., values, improving the relationship, reducing hostility) may be discussed.
- *Seek forgiveness*: The transgressor seeks forgiveness, often by

expressing remorse, apologizing sincerely and (in some cases) offering compensation.

- *Grant/accept forgiveness:* The victim may signal a willingness to forgive. Forgiveness may be granted conditionally, often under the assurance that the transgression will not be repeated, or unconditionally. Although under no obligation to do so, the victim begins to "let go" of at least some of the negative emotion harbored toward the offender. They forgo the right to seek revenge.
- *Renegotiate rules and values:* The parties renegotiate the rules of the relationship with the goal of finding a framework that is just, fair, and safe. In some cases the relationship is terminated, downgraded, formalized, or subjected to supervision.
- *Monitor relational transition:* As time unfolds, the parties monitor compliance with the renegotiated rules and values. Depending on this assessment, the forgiveness process may be revisited, reconciliation may be attempted, or the parties may persist with the new relationship guidelines.

Conclusion

So the fundamental question is, what sort of relationship is forged between people and their employers within the workplace, the place where people spend so much time?

Pfeffer, 2009: 384

Organizational scholar Jeffrey Pfeffer (2009) makes a compelling case that employees are becoming increasingly alienated from their organizations. His reading of national surveys and business trends suggests that job-satisfaction levels are in a free fall, employees are less trusting of their employers, and many are growing reluctant to invest their creativity and effort in organizations they perceive to be indifferent or even exploitative. All of this is happening at a time when the work week continues to lengthen, employee benefits are in decline, and job security remains fragile. Against this backdrop of a fraying employee–employer relationship, Pfeffer argues that what employees are seeking from work is a sense of community – a feeling of belonging to a caring group of people who share responsibility, agree on core values, and commit to long-term relationships.

Pfeffer may be naive in this view. After all, many employees relish the role of "free agent," moving from job to job as new challenges arise and economic opportunities present themselves. Many of us are perfectly happy to find a sense of belonging online, locating like-minded friends in the vast virtual communities of the Internet. Still others are content to make their social connections in faith communities or through their recreational pursuits. Still, I think Pfeffer may be on to something. Some of the most successful organizations in the Western world are known for building workplace community: Southwest Airlines, Costco, and AirBus (the European aircraft manufacturer). What makes these organizations communal? They tend to make long-term commitments to employees and sustain them through difficult economic times. They view employees as whole people and provide the flexibility and benefits that help employees with work–life balance. They encourage employee camaraderie and mutual support. In return, employees tend to be committed, creative, and highly productive.

Many less communal organizations are also economically successful. Their relationships with employees are tenuous, distant, and legalistic. The short-term profit picture and the interests of stockholders are their primary concerns. On the list of organizational priorities, these economic considerations are placed well ahead of employee well-being. But it does appear that at least some employees have grown weary of this culture of mutual exploitation. And it may be that communal organizations reap competitive benefit when employees truly "buy-in" to organizational values and link their own success to that of the company's long term prospects. As Pfeffer argues, organizations have a choice to make and many of those who chose a more communal approach have been undeniably successful.

Organizations are many things, but perhaps most fundamentally, they are networks of human relationships. Even in this technological age, the computers cease to whir and business plans fall flat when the people in charge of them fail to communicate, cooperate, and care about their collective fate. In this chapter, and throughout this book, I have made the case that emotion is a key indicator of relationship quality. It conveys important information about the status of the bonds that connect organizations with their public stakeholders, employees with their employers, and co-worker with co-worker. If organizations are to become more communal, they will need to monitor more closely the emotional benefits and costs of decisions and policies. They will honor the emotional investments that employees make in jobs, co-workers, and the organization itself. They will acknowledge that the emotional implications of work extend beyond the boundaries of the organization, deep into the personal relationships of employees.

In chapter 1, I suggested that emotion can be conceptualized from numerous points of view, but among the most compelling is the idea that emotional communication evolved as an important facilitator of social cooperation in complex organizations. But, I argued, the communication of emotion is more than a survival mechanism. It motivates employees to do their best work, helps them forge meaningful relationships, and alerts them to danger and wrongdoing. Emotion can be manipulated and, when expressed without care for others, it can be harmful. But I make the case that emotional communication has the potential to help organizations and individual workers flourish. It helps us do good.

Chapter 2 detailed the many forms that emotional communication can take at the various levels of organization. Emotion is connected to communication in myriad ways: emotional experiences motivate employees to communicate (or not); emotional communication competencies facilitate the success of some employees; organizations and cultures regulate the expression of emotion by establishing communication rules; organizational messages, structures, and technologies shape the emotions of employees and various stakeholders, intentionally or unintentionally. Chapter 3 examined how these processes of emotional communication are performed by members of various occupations, and chapter 4 traces their role in sustaining workplace relationships. Chapter

5 developed the idea that emotional communication can be used for good (or bad) organizational purposes. It chronicled the central role of the moral emotions as guides to ethical workplace behavior.

This final chapter explored a variety of developing trends, some of which employees are already well aware. The chapter is intended to leave the reader pondering both the dark and the bright sides of emotional communication in the evolving workplace. Some trends are unquestionably discouraging. At this moment, Western culture really does seem to be cultivating a climate of callousness and this is reflected in the workplace experiences of many employees. I also find discouraging the trends toward continual connectivity and temporary work relationships, because these arrangements make it difficult to cultivate emotionally rich connections among co-workers. But this angst reflects my own preference for communal, rather than simply contractual, forms of organization.

Other trends are encouraging. Social media offer possibilities for workers to sustain long-term connections despite the relation-ship-disrupting effects of layoffs or temporary work assignments. Emerging technologies are prompting workers to think about the emotional implication of their messages and making mediated forms of communication more emotionally nuanced. I find hope in the increasing interests that social scientists are showing in posi-tive emotions, such as, well, *hope*. This is reflected in new thinking about the applicability of forgiveness processes to the workplace. Forgiveness has been incorporated in efforts to promote healing after some of the world's most distressing and intractable conflicts. Surely it can be useful in redressing the hurt and wrongdoing that people experience in their working lives.

Perhaps the most encouraging trend is that researchers and prac-titioners are becoming more attuned to the emotional dimensions of work. No longer is the workplace considered a bastion of cool rationality or dispassionate professionalism. The communication practices and organizational consequences of emotional commu-nication are receiving greater attention. The role of emotion in vitalizing and humanizing the workplace is more fully acknowl-edged now then it was just a few years ago. On the whole, I am inclined to think, and, of course, *to feel*, that this is a good thing, for both organizations and their employees.

References

Analoui, F. (1995). Workplace sabotage: its styles, motives and management. *Journal of Management Development*, 14: 48–65.

Carr, N. (2010). *The Shallows: What the Internet is Doing to Our Brain*. New York: W.W. Norton.

Chatfield, T. (2010). Why playing in the virtual world has an awful lot to teach children (January 10). Retrieved from *The Observer* website: <http://www.guardian.co.uk/technology/2010/jan/10/playing-in-the-virtual-world>.

Concordia University (2008). New image processing system detects moods. *ScienceDaily* (December 4). Retrieved August 3, 2010, from: <http://www.sciencedaily.com /releases/2008/12/081202133232.htm>.

Conley, D. (2009). *Elsewhere, U.S.A.: How We Got from the Company Man, Family Dinners, and the Affluent Society to the Home Office, BlackBerry Moms, and Economic Anxiety*. New York: Pantheon.

de Becker, G. (1997). *The Gift of Fear and Other Survival Signals that Protect Us from Violence*. New York: Dell Publishing.

de Cuyper, N., and de Witt, H. (2008). Volition and reasons for accepting temporary employment: associations with attitudes, well-being, and behavioural intentions. *European Journal of Work and Organizational Psychology*, 17: 363–87.

Escoffery, D. S. (ed.) (2006). *How Real is Reality TV? Essays on Representation and Truth*. Jefferson, NC: McFarland,

Fineman, S. (ed.). (2000). *Emotion in Organizations* (2nd edn). London: Sage.

Fitzpatrick, L. (2010). We're getting off the ladder. *Time*, 173(20) (May 25): 45.

Flandez, R. (2009). Small businesses work hard to prevent layoffs. Retrieved from the *Wall Street Journal* website: <http://online.wsj.com/article/NA_WSJ_PUB:SB123620703459133563.html>.

Franko, E. M. (2006). Democracy in the workplace? The Lessons of Donald Trump and *The Apprentice*. In D. S. Escoffery (ed.), *How Real is Reality TV? Essays on Representation and Truth*. Jefferson, NC: McFarland, pp. 247–58.

Gentile, D. A., Lynch P. J., Linder, J. R., and Walsh, D. A (2003). The effects of violent video game habits on adolescent hostility, aggressive behaviors, and school performance. *Journal of Adolescence*, 27: 5–22.

Greenberg, J. (ed.) (2010). *Insidious Workplace Behavior*. New York: Routledge.

Hartford Courant (2010). 9 Dead in Manchester, Conn. workplace shooting (August 3). Retrieved from: <http://articles.courant.com>.

Hegstrom, T. G. (1999). Reasons for rocking the boat: principles and personal problems. In H. K. Geissner, A. F. Herbig, and E. Wessela (eds), *Business Communication in Europe*. Tostedt, Germany: Attikon Verlag, pp. 179–94.

Hochschild, A. (1983). *The Managed Heart*. Berkeley, CA: University of California Press.

Jefferson, T. (1818; 1903). [Letter to John Adams, November 13] In A. A. Lipscomb, A. E. Bergh, R. H. Johnson (eds), *The Writings of Thomas Jefferson, Volume 15*. Washington, DC: Thomas Jefferson Memorial Association of the United States. Also retrieved from: <http://www.beliefnet.com/resourcelib/docs/55/Letter_from_Thomas_Jefferson_to_John_Adams_1.html>.

Judge, T. A., Ilies, R., and Scott, B. R. (2005). Work–family conflict and emotions: effects at work and at home. *International Journal of Work, Organisation, and Emotion*, 1: 4–19.

Kassing, J. W. (1997). Articulating, antagonizing, and displacing: a model of employee dissent. *Communication Studies*, 48: 311–32.

Kelan, E. (2008). Bound by stereotypes. *Business Strategy Review*, 19: 4–7.

Kiviat, B. (2009). After layoffs, there's survivor's guilt. *Time* (February 1). Retrieved from magazine website: <http://www.time.com/time/business/article/0,8599,1874592,00.html>.

Kunda, G., Barley, S. R., and Evans, J. (2002). Why do contractors contract? The experience of highly skilled technical professionals in a contingent labor market. *Industrial and Labor Relations Review*, 55: 234–57.

Levine, L. (2009). Unemployment through layoff: what are the reasons? Retrieved from *Key Work Documents: Federal Publications* website (Ithaca, NY: Cornell University): <http://digitalcommons.ilr.cornell.edu/cgi/viewcontent.cgi?article=1190andcontext=key_workplace>.

Lorenzo-Dus, N. (2008). Real disorder in the court: an investigation of conflict talk in U.S. television courtroom shows. *Media, Culture, and Society*, 30: 81–107.

Lutgen-Sandvik, P., Namie, G., and Namie, R. (2009). Workplace bullying: causes, consequences, and corrections. In P. Lutgen-Sandvik and B. Sypher (eds), *Destructive Organizational Communication: Processes, Consequences, and Constructive Ways of Organizing*. New York: Routledge, pp. 27–52.

Mayerowitz, S. (2010). Angry JetBlue flight attendant flees plane at JFK airport via emergency slide. Retrieved from the ABC News website: <http://abcnews.go.com/US/jetblue-flight-attendant-steven-slater-arrested-flight-jfk/story?id=11361298>.

Metts, S., Cupach, W. R., and Lippert, L. (2006). Forgiveness in the workplace. In J. M. Harden-Fritz and B. L. Ohmdahl (eds), *Problematic Relationships in the Workplace*. New York: Peter Lang Publishing, pp. 249–78.

Morin, R., and Kochhar, R. (2010). Lost income, lost friends – and loss of self-respect. Retrieved from the Pew Research Center website: <http://pewresearch.org/pubs/1674/poll-impact-long-term-unemployment>.

Mosaic Threat Assessment Systems (2010). Retrieved from: <https://www.mosaicmethod.com/>.

Patterson, T. (2009). *Welcome to the "Weisure" Lifestyle*. Retrieved July

31, 2010, from: <http://www.cnn.com/2009/LIVING/worklife/05/11/weisure/index.html?iref=newssearch>.

Pfeffer, J. (2009). Working alone: whatever happened to organizations as communities? In P. Lutgen-Sandvik and B. Sypher (eds), *Destructive Organizational Communication: Processes, Consequences, and Constructive Ways of Organizing*. New York: Routledge, pp. 363–88. Reprinted from E. E. Lawler II, and J. O'Toole (eds), *America at Work: Choices and Challenges*. New York: Palgrave Macmillan, 2006.

Rivera, R., and Robbins, L. (2010). Troubles preceded Connecticut workplace killing, Retrieved 5 August, 2010, from the *New York Times* website: <http://www.nytimes.com/2010/08/04/nyregion/04shooting.html?ref=connecticut>.

Sullivan, S. E. (1999). The changing nature of careers: a review and research agenda. *Journal of Management*, 25: 457–84.

United States Bureau of Labor Statistics (2005). *Contingent and Alternative Work Arrangements*. Retrieved August 1, 2010, from: <http://www.bls.gov/news.release/pdf/conemp.pdf>.

United States Bureau of Labor (2010a). *Occupational Outlook Handbook, 2010–2011 Edition*. Retrieved from: <http://www.bls.gov/oco/oco2003.htm#employment>.

United States Bureau of Labor (2010b). *The Employment Situation – June 2010*. At: <http://www.bls.gov/news.release/pdf/empsit.pdf>.

United States Patent and Trade Office (2007). USPTO Deputy Director Peterlin testifies at House Committee hearing on telework. Retrieved at: <http://www.uspto.gov/news/pr/2007/07-45.jsp>.

Waldron, V. (2000). Relational experiences and emotion at work. In S. Fineman (ed.), *Emotion in Organizations* (2nd edn). London, Sage, pp. 64–82.

Waldron, V., and Kelley, D. (2008). *Communicating Forgiveness*. Thousand Oaks, CA: Sage.

Waldron, V., and Krone, K. J. (1991). The experience and expression of emotion in the workplace: a study of a corrections organization. *Management Communication Quarterly*, 4: 287–309.

Index

Index

Index